When I ~~was a lad in Saltburn~~

Best wishes
Paul Duffin

by
Paul Duffin

Cover design by Claire Duffin

©2019 Paul Duffin

Other books by Paul Duffin

NOT TOO BAD (Nov 2016)

From the 1970's diaries of a teenage Brummie
All proceeds to Guide Dogs

"Enjoy this sparkling piece of modern-day local history made fun" JH

AND THE CRICKET WAS GOOD TOO! (Nov 2017)

Enjoy the fun and laughter following the England cricket team around the world on nine of their tours.
All proceeds to Sense, the Deafblind charity

"You don't have to be a cricket fan to enjoy this book"
Anon

"An enjoyable read full of laughs"
The Cricketer Magazine May 2018

SAY THE LEEDS AND YOU'RE SMILING (Nov 2018)

Anyone who thinks working in an office is boring will think otherwise as they read about the fun and games we experienced at the Leeds Permanent Building society
All proceeds to Prostate Cancer UK

"H. G. Wells couldn't have done it better"
Dave G

Available on Amazon in Kindle and paperback

Preface

This is my fourth self-published book with all proceeds donated to charity. This time the Alzheimer's charity will benefit. Both my Mom and her sister (Aunt Joyce) suffered from this disease but lived to good ages with Mom reaching 90 and Aunt Joyce 87. The first two books helped charities connected with my severe sight and hearing impairment i.e. Guide Dogs and Sense (the deafblind charity). The third book supported Prostate Cancer UK. Total funds raised have now passed £4000.

This book draws on my experience of growing up from the latter part of the 1950s up to my 'O' level year (1970) in the Birmingham suburb of Yardley. I am a truly baby booming Brummie.

I hope readers find the comparison of those times with the modern world both interesting and at times amusing. Older readers will I am sure find themselves taken back to a very different era, with Brummies recognising places and institutions many of which have now disappeared.

Many people have helped me remember those times particularly friends I grew up with such as John Lavender and Gary Durant. A big thank you to my regular "editors" Liz Lavender and Andy Bates who played vital roles in the book's production. My wife Sue (also a Brummie) helpfully reviewed each chapter along the way. I must also thank my friends and family for their support and patience as I constantly mentioned "the book".

Introduction

My Mom's parents, John and Emma Piggott, met and married in West Bromwich in the summer of 1920. Both their parents were iron puddlers (converting pig iron into wrought iron) and Grandad John carried on in the family tradition. My Dad's folks, however, Harold and Beatrice Duffin were born and raised in Nottingham but moved to Alum Rock in Brum just after the end of the First World War and were married in 1919. Both sets of parents had their first born almost exactly one year after marriage; Dad Harold Stanley (Stan) in November 1920 and Mom Olive in May 1921.

My Mom met my Dad just before the outbreak of war whilst working in the offices of the Birmingham Co-operative Society on the High Street in the city centre.

Dad was called up by the RAF in 1941 at the age of 20 yrs leaving my Mom to be moved to a munitions factory and face regular air raids. They married in June 1943 honeymooning in Broadstairs. Dad was demobbed in 1946 after spending much of his time in Egypt which he did not like despite missing any real action which had ended by the time he arrived.

They bought a terraced house in Freer Road on the Aston/Handsworth border just ten minutes' walk down Birchfield Road to my Mom's parents in Alma Street Aston. My brother, Stephen, was born in February 1950. I followed three and a half years later in September 1953. Within a year we had moved to a three bed semi in Charminster Avenue, just off Stoney lane, close to the Yew Tree area in Yardley. My Dad was a keen cricketer and useful tennis player and I think their property choice was swayed by its proximity to the excellent facilities provided by his employer's sports ground in Barrows Lane about a fifteen minute walk from our new home.

Britain was a very different country in the early 1950's. The impact of the war was still being felt with rationing continuing until just two months before my birth. The economy was struggling with the standard rate of income tax at 43%, more than twice the current basic rate. Pollution was a real problem with the reliance on coal leading to dangerous smogs hitting major cities such as Birmingham.

The 1951 census recorded the population at 50 million of whom 3%were born overseas with the largest groups from Ireland (500,000) and Poland (160,000). The NHS was still in its infancy having been launched in 1946.

Like most people I can't remember much if anything before the age of four so I will pick up from 1957.

Chapter 1 1957:   Home

Side Splitting

My earliest recollection is one of excruciating pain. All I can really remember is that I was four years old and my midriff was on fire! I must have been rushed to hospital because before I knew it, I was lying in Selly Oak Hospital trying to work out what was going on. It turned out I had suffered acute appendicitis. The offending tissue was removed and although I was certainly sore the dreadful pain and nausea had thankfully gone.

Selly Oak Hospital, located to the south west of Birmingham city centre, wasn't exactly state of the art, not that I really noticed at that tender age. Originally a workhouse infirmary opening for 300 patients in 1897 at a cost of £45,000 it became part of the NHS in 1948. By 2001 it was a home for injured military servicemen, finally closing in 2011 when the hospital services were transferred to the Queen Elizabeth Hospital in the city centre.

There were some benefits to my suffering as gifts soon began to arrive. I received a Western annual from our neighbours, the Peacocks, who lived attached to us at number 7, and plenty of sweets from other well-wishers. Much to my dismay however, my stack of sweets was instantly removed by a nurse who informed me that "all sweets are shared here". I was never sure that I got my fair share.

I also remember the boy in the bed next to me. I never found out his name or what had happened to him but was fascinated to discover that he had both legs in plaster with an extra section forming an H-like link between them. How was he ever going to walk like that? Maybe he couldn't walk but there was nothing wrong with his arms as he made sure he had his fair share of the sweets.

After my surgery I spent several days recovering and struggling to come to terms with the sweet sharing rule. Eventually I was discharged home to continue recovery there. I had been back a couple of days and was being minded by our other neighbours, the lovely Beresfords (at number 11) whilst my Mom was at the laundrette on Hobmoor Road. Suddenly I felt a resurgence of pain and was soon in agony all over again. Mom was quickly recalled and an ambulance summoned to take me back to hospital where it was discovered that I had developed an infection as a result of the surgery. More sweet sharing but the antibiotics soon did the trick and I was back home within a few days.

At four years old I was proud to show everyone my impressive "war wound". Sixty years later the criss-cross stitch marks have long since gone, although the care and attention I received from staff and neighbours has left a warm glow.

Home Sweet Home

We lived at number 9 Charminster Avenue, one of three roads that made up "The Square" just off Stoney Lane close to the Yew Tree in Yardley, a "blue collar" Birmingham suburb. The Square was bordered by Charminster Avenue and Rockingham Road each forming one side, and Heathmere Avenue which formed the other two sides. There were just over 100 houses almost all of which were three bedroom semis built by Dares in the late 1930s. Dare H and son were based in Alum Rock and built hundreds of house in Birmingham. Harry Dare became a director of Birmingham City football club and his firm built one of the stands. 9, Charminster was a Dare's house built in 1938/9. All the houses had front and back gardens; most also had a garage and a shared drive even though very few housed cars back then.

Directly opposite our house was a former bomb site where in November 1940, during one of the most intense air raids, two houses were destroyed and three people were killed. Unfortunately, one of the victims was a young woman who had been bombed out of her house a few days earlier and was fatally bombed whilst staying with friends.

The hub of our home was the living room where we basically "lived". It had a dining table with a drop leaf, a sideboard crammed with anything and everything from shoes and knitting to best crockery. A couple of easy chairs were squeezed in front of the coal fire. A rather exotic feature were the French windows leading into the garden although I can never remember them actually being opened, mainly because they were blocked by the dining table. About 18 inches below the ceiling there was a picture rail that ran around the room but was never used to hang any pictures. These appeared in most of the rooms but were treated as part of the decoration and the wooden rails were painted to match the colour scheme.

Our first TV arrived to coincide with my dad's football team, Aston Villa, reaching and then winning the FA cup. Sadly, I have no recollection of the match. The black and white set only received BBC and the valves were in frequent need of replacement, which meant a visit to Radio Rentals on Church Road to report the fault. Most people rented their sets due to high cost of buying their own.

The lounge (front room) was used for best, which meant hardly ever. It was larger than the living room as it had a bay window. It also benefitted from the late afternoon sun making its lack of use even more surprising. Both downstairs rooms had coal fires which probably explained why the lounge room was seldom used at this point.

The kitchen was tiny and could only boast a white ceramic sink and basic Creda gas cooker. We had no fridge or washer so Mom had to store our food in the pantry under the stairs with the cold tiled floor helping only slightly to keep things cool. Like almost everyone on The Square she visited the laundrette once a week with occasional visits to the laundry on Church Road for bigger items, which would be returned neatly wrapped in brown paper and tied up with string (one of my favourite things!). We wouldn't have any fancy appliances for at least the next ten years.

Upstairs at 9 Charminster there were two double bedrooms, a box room, a bathroom and a separate toilet. There was no heating upstairs. Although the two main rooms had open fires, I can't remember them ever being lit. The bathroom had a hot water tank that only ever got hot when the immersion heater was switched on. This was a costly affair, so the switch only ever went down after careful consideration.

Oh Boy that bedroom I shared with my older brother Steve was cold in the winter, and yes there were times when ice formed on the inside of the windows, but the experience was certainly not out of the ordinary amongst my peers. The box room had two outside walls making it even colder, so it was used for storage for many years until Steve needed his own space. His yearning for independence must have been strong for him to brave the "ice box". It housed a large basket containing the remains of unused wallpaper rolls. Apparently, this was originally my "cot".

Each room had lino (no one used the correct term, linoleum) flooring with a square of carpet laid on top. Fitted carpet would not arrive for a number of years. The hall had small black and white tiles partially covered with two red rugs, presumably to provide some warmth, as well as some fun for us boys. Steve and I would run up and skid along on the rugs when Mom's eyes were focused elsewhere.

We also used the hall for a game featuring a balloon and the frames of the front door and the kitchen door as "goals". The windows in the hall and on the landing had tiny panes of coloured glass plus larger leaded frosted panes. This would later strike me as out of keeping with the rest of the house.

Smoke Gets in Your Eyes and Lungs

The reliance on coal for heating the living room and lounge meant a regular visit from the coal man whose bags were tipped into the coal shed located just outside the kitchen window in the back garden. On top of the bunker was a failed attempt to grow plants. The only thing which seemed to grow was clover which almost entirely covered the flat roof. Many hours were spent searching for, and occasionally securing, the elusive four-leaf variety. Oh, how lucky we were!

One of the drawbacks from the heavy use of coal across the country was the resulting pollution. London had suffered severe smogs in 1952 lasting several days. Birmingham also fell victim and along with other industrial cities benefitted tremendously from the introduction of the Clean Air Act in 1956. This led to Yardley being included in a smokeless zone that meant we could only burn smokeless coal such as Coalite. We still suffered a few smogs for a while and I can remember being told to breathe through my handkerchief which left a disconcerting yellow stain.

Our back garden had two small lawns. The smaller of the two ran alongside the asbestos garage which was used for storage and garden tools. There were then three steps down to the larger lower lawn. This was twice the size of the very small top lawn at about twelve feet square and therefore the venue for many hours of play. Even with me at four and brother Steve aged seven, Dad was keen to develop our ball skills. I really enjoyed those precious times with Dad.

Pre school

It would be another year before I started school and began to make friends, but it was around this time that I met my oldest friend John Lavender. John lived at number 12 Rockingham road with his older brother Martin and his Mom and Dad, Doreen and Arthur. According to my Mom (Brummies tend to opt for Mom in preference to Mum) we first met in the doctors' waiting room and have remained good friends ever since despite living 200 miles or more apart. I would soon meet and befriend many others from all around the square and beyond.

On patrol

The neighbourhood was very friendly. Very few people had cars so had to get about on foot or use public transport. This led to a lot of social interaction. There was only one exit from the square on to Stoney Lane. Whenever we headed out of the square we had to negotiate our way past two danger points. Cissy Eccles regularly patrolled the front garden of number 3 Charminster waiting to snare passing folk for a long chat. Just around the corner from her, on the way out of The Square another trap was set by Mrs Brown at 5 Rockingham Road. She was often dressed in her pink house coat regardless of the weather, with a cigarette never far from her mouth. My Mom made no real effort to avoid either of these ladies as they were a very useful source of local information, not gossip of course. I would often stand bored shifting my weight from one side to the other urging Mom to move on.

Christmas Surprise

Mom and Dad always made Christmas special for Steve and me despite their limited funds. Even the lounge came into full use at this time of year as it housed the Christmas tree which was decorated and lit with real candles. My 1957 Christmas was especially memorable as in addition to a pillowcase containing oranges and chocolate coins wrapped in gold coloured foil, I was delighted to receive a TRICYCLE!

It was red with white mudguards and very smart even if it was not brand new (none of my bikes ever were). I was so excited and couldn't wait for my Dad to carry it downstairs and let me out in the cold to try it out.

I am pretty sure we all would have been seated in front of our tiny television for the Queen's first televised Christmas speech of which, not surprisingly, I have absolutely no recollection. Sorry Ma'am.

Amongst the presents was one I didn't appreciate for some time was a Premium Bond. Premium Bonds were introduced by Prime Minister Harold Macmillan at the end of the previous year to help stem inflation and encourage saving. Grandma Piggott (my Mom's Mom) bought Steve and I one each. I still have mine over 60 years later and I'm still waiting for the big one. Come on Ernie.

Other Events in 1957

9 January – Harold Macmillan succeeds Anthony Eden as Prime Minister

16 January-The Cavern Club opens in Liverpool as a jazz club

16 February - the "Toddlers' Truce" (an arrangement whereby there were no television broadcasts between 18:00-19:00 to allow parents to put their children to bed) is abolished

24 April – first broadcast of BBC Television astronomy series The Sky at Night presented by Patrick Moore

4 May – Aston Villa win the FA Cup for a record seventh time with a 2-1 win over Manchester United

14 May – end of petrol rationing following the Suez Crisis

15 May -- Stanley Matthews plays his final international soccer game

27 June – a report by the Medical Research Council reveals that there is evidence to support a link between tobacco smoking and lung cancer

6 July – future members of The Beatles John Lennon and Paul McCartney first meet as teenagers

20 July - Prime Minister Harold Macmillan makes an optimistic speech; "most of our people have never had it so good"

5 August – the cartoon character Andy Capp first appears in northern editions of the Daily Mirror

10 September – Tony Lock becomes the last bowler to reach 200 wickets in a first-class season

30 October – the Government unveils plans which will allow women to join the House of Lords for the first time

Best-selling single in 1957; Diana – Paul Anka

Chapter 2 1958: All hooked up

Sporting challenge

My Dad was a keen sportsman and had won several awards for cricket and tennis. He had also won a high jump competition whilst serving with the RAF in Egypt during the Second World War. In April 1958 he was appointed Playing Fields and Social Club Secretary at the Co-op sports club in Barrows Lane Yardley. This was a part time position which he held in addition to his daytime role as Chief Clerk in the Co-op Accounts Department located above the department store in the High Street of the city centre. I am sure the extra money would have helped but it was a shame that he would be forced to spend more time away from home. I was too young to understand but I am sure he would have missed the lost time with us too.

The playing fields were only about a fifteen-minute walk from our home along Stoney Lane to the Yew Tree turning left up Church Road, past the Ring O' Bells, finally turning right into Barrows Lane. The whole family, including Grandpa and Nana Duffin, spent time at the playing fields. My grandparents were keen crown green bowls players. There were three cricket pitches, two crown green bowling greens and at least half a dozen tennis courts. Archery was also available but rarely were budding Robin Hoods seen on the green.

Although it was a relatively short walk my Dad soon got tired of the jaunt and purchased a moped which would help cut down the time spent away from home. Can't say it was a "funky" moped because it wasn't, but it was practical and when not in use lived in the garage. Steve and I were never allowed to ride on the back and I am not even sure if it had passenger capability.

Party time

A requirement of Dad's new part time role was the installation of a telephone in case of emergencies at the club. There was great excitement in the Duffin household when the GPO came to hook us up with the black Bakelite phone. We had a telegraph pole right outside our front garden wall which was a bit of a surprise as so very few homes had phones in the mid-1950s.

Neither sets of grandparents or any of our relatives had phones. Who would call us, and who would we ring?
My Mom tried to explain to us that we should not touch the new equipment. If it rang, we should leave it to the grown-ups to answer. What I later discovered was that we had been given a "party line". This meant that we shared a line with Mary and Reg Tranter who lived opposite us in a recently re-built semi on what was a bomb site. If the Tranters were using the line you could pick up our phone and hear every word. They of course could do the same.

Communication breakdown

The lack of the ability to communicate with friends and family was something the current generation would find hard to appreciate. Planning was essential, a skill which has almost disappeared as smart phones and the internet make instant decision making and frequent change of plans the norm.

There were two red phone boxes at the Yew Tree. Not that they were used much as no one had anyone to phone. There was a choice of two buttons to press, marked A and B. You pressed button A to speak and button B to get your money back if no one answered.

The dials on all phones carried letters as well as numbers. Our phone number was STE 3733. The STE stood for the Stechford area. Later the letters were replaced by numbers with STE becoming 783.

Back at home Steve and I quickly learnt that there was a way of playing a trick on Mom and Dad. You could dial 'FRB', scurry into the living room and wait for the phone to ring. When the phone was picked up there would be no one on the line of course, as it was just a testing facility. This caused Mom and Dad to be initially confused and later, when they worked out what Steve and I were up to, a certain annoyance. We of course found it hilarious.

One or the other

When it came to choosing a primary school my parents had two options: Hobmoor Primary which was located a matter of yards away as the playground backed on to Rockingham Road or Church road Primary just past the Yew Tree. There was still a yew tree planted close to the roundabout outside the Yew Tree public house. The entrance to Hobmoor was at least a ten minute walk up to the Yew Tree then back down Hobmoor Road to the turning just past the W & HO fishing tackle shop. The entrance to Church Road was a similar distance but meant crossing the busy Church Road. The split between the schools was about equal amongst the children around the square. Both schools had good reputations with Church Road being much larger having at least three classes for each year as opposed to just one class per year at Hobmoor.

When Steve started school just after we moved to Yardley in 1954, Hobmoor got the vote. It was therefore only natural that I followed in my big brother's footsteps.
Hobmoor was built in the late 1920's. We knew this because there was a plaque celebrating the opening situated on the wall of the caretaker's house close to the entrance. Facilities were fairly basic evidenced by the open-air boy's toilets. The wall was often used to record boys reaching new heights.

The old wooden desks in some classrooms still had ink wells. These had not been used for some time and were as dried up as some of the 'shipped in' school dinners.

Living so close to the school meant that I was fortunate enough to walk home with Steve for lunch where I was often greeted with a plate of mashed potato topped with a poached egg or the contents from a tin of Cross and Blackwell scotch broth.

Morris for this minor

On Monday 7th September 1958 I entered a whole new world led at class one level by Miss Morris the reception class teacher. There were seven classes at Hobmoor Primary which, when I was there, were taught by Miss Trotter who also played the piano, Mrs Wilcox (the grumpy deputy head), Mrs Miller, Miss Wright (my favourite who read such lovely stories to us), Mr Hughes who also ran the sports teams, and a very strict Mr Brooks. In addition, there was a remedial class (an early version of special needs) run by Miss Scott. The Headmistress was a very quiet Miss Pargeter who was ably assisted by Mrs Roberts the school secretary who ran the tuck shop at lunch time.

Of the 45 pupils the boys were easily in the minority. This didn't really matter until we had to field football and cricket teams against local schools with more lads to choose from. Prior to me starting school my Mom had spent lots of time helping me with reading and doing very basic sums. I was one of the eldest in our huge class of 45 as my fifth birthday was just a week after I started. This meant I had a significant age advantage over other pupils in the same class who had just turned four. I soon got to grips with Janet and John Book One and was off and running, well reading actually.

Time to go home

I can remember enjoying my first term making new friends such as Nigel Osgood and Peter Sceney both from the square and being part of a large group.

However, I also missed the daily routine of "watching with mother" (WWM) each day after lunch. It was scheduled for 1.30pm which clashed with my return to school as I only had about 40 minutes at home for lunch. The WWM schedule in 1958 was:

Monday - Picture Book

This was my least favourite of the Watch with Mother programmes. It encouraged children to make things but there was no mention of sticky backed plastic. It was originally presented by Patricia Driscoll who left in 1957 to play Maid Marian in ITV's 'Adventures of Robin Hood'. As we could only get BBC on our television, we had to wait until we had Sunday tea at Grandpa Duffin's to catch up with the thrills and spills in Sherwood Forest. Picture Book was eventually replaced by Camberwick Green in 1966.

Tuesday - Andy Pandy

I liked Andy Pandy and was always ready to give him a wave. Andy lived in a basket and was often joined by Teddy and a rag doll called Looby Loo. Originally the programme was broadcast live but it wasn't long before some bright spark at the Beeb realised that filming episodes would allow repeats to be shown. The BBC made full use of this facility as the 26 filmed episodes were repeated from 1952 to 1969 when it was eventually "time to go home" with Andy waving goodbye.

Wednesday - Flower Pot Men

Bill and Ben were two little men made of flower pots who lived at the bottom of the garden. Little Weed grew between the pots. The Flowerpot men spoke their own language called 'oddle poddle'. For example "Slobadob"was their way of saying "Slowcoach" the garden tortoise. This language was invented by Peter Hawkins who also invented the voices of the Daleks and Captain Pugwash.

Each Bill and Ben episode ended with the unseen approach of the gardener and the pots saying "babap icckle weed".

Thursday - Rag, Tag and Bobtail

Rag was a hedgehog, Tag a mouse and Bobtail a rabbit. The three glove puppets didn't really get up to much but they must have done something as the 26 episodes were recycled for twelve years before finally being replaced by Tales of the Riverbank in 1965.

Friday - The Wooden Tops

This was my favourite. The Wooden Top family featured Mummy, Daddy, twins Jenny and Willy, baby and of course the star, Spotty Dog. This was the biggest spotty dog you ever did see! There were also 26 episodes of the programme which was designed to promote family life and ran until 1973.

Other events in 1958

6 February – The plane carrying the Manchester Utd team crashes at Munich killing 23

25 February – Bertrand Russell launches the Campaign for Nuclear Disarmament (CND)

24 March – work on the M1, Britain's first full length motorway, begins

4–7 April – the first protest march for the Campaign for Nuclear Disarmament from Hyde Park, London to Aldermarston

22 April – the Hancock's Half Hour episode "Sunday Afternoon at Home" is first broadcast on BBC radio. When I later became a Hancock fan this was my favourite episode

4 June – the Duke of Edinburgh's Award presented for the first time at Buckingham Palace

9 June – the Queen officially reopens Gatwick Airport, which has been expanded at a cost of more than £7,000,000

10 July – first parking meters installed in the UK

18–26 July – British Empire and Commonwealth Games held in Cardiff

24 July – the first life peerage is created

26 July - Abolition of the presentation of débutantes to the royal court

1 August - Premiere of Carry on Sergeant, the first Carry On film

29 August - release of Cliff Richard's debut single

30 August - Notting Hill race riots in London

1 September – the first Cod War between UK and Iceland breaks out
10 November – Donald Campbell sets the world water speed record at 248.62 mph

5 December-The Preston Bypass, the UK's first motorway, is opened by Prime Minister Harold Macmillan
Best-selling single in 1958 – Jailhouse Rock by Elvis Presley

Chapter 3 1959:   Ride 'em Cowboy

Everything stops for tea

Sunday tea was often spent at Grandpa and Nannah Duffin's. Although it was less than two miles as the crow flies to 58 Jephcott Road Alum Rock, it would take two buses and up to an hour with Sunday bus timetables. The stop for the Outer Circle number 11 was just around the corner on Stoney Lane. We would get off just past the Bull's Head pub in Stechford and catch the number 14 to the top of Jephcott Road on Cotterills Lane.

My grandparents had lived in their three-bedroom council house from when it was built in about 1922. It had a good-sized living room that housed a piano, drop leafed dining table and three piece suite. There was just enough room for Joey the budgie's cage from which he constantly repeated "who's a pretty boy".

Out the back was the kitchen and a bathroom containing just a bath. Strangely you had to go outside to enter the toilet which was part of the house but with no internal access. Upstairs were two double bedrooms with beds so high you almost needed a ladder to gain entry. There was also a small box room for storage but no bathroom.

Sunday teas were all very similar. Ham or tongue (I wasn't keen on the latter) with salad, followed by tinned orange segments with evaporated milk. Finished off with homemade buns or cake and a cup of tea to swill them down. If we were good, we could watch TV as they had ITV and Robin Hood was a must. We would often play cards or listen to 78rpm records with "the quartermaster's store" being my favourite.

The visit finished with cocoa or Camp coffee before falling asleep on the bus on the way home. On saying goodbye we would always be offered a florin (a 2 shilling piece= 10p) or a half crown (2/6 =12.5p). We would politely decline then readily accept as the offer was repeated.

The Duffins were good fun, especially Grandpa Duffin. He joined up within days of the outbreak of WW1 in 1914, being eventually invalided out in 1918. His left arm was hit by shrapnel leaving him unable to use two of the fingers of his left hand. He had a great sense of humour and was always smiling. He never lost his temper and was always interested in life. He loved dancing and all kinds of music. He was a very good bowls player, both indoor and crown green, winning several trophies. Nannah was quite quiet but very supportive. During the war she found the bombing very stressful and had "suffered with her nerves".

At home with the Piggotts

Trips to the Piggotts (Mom's parents) were far less frequent due mainly to an even more difficult journey to the other side of town. 25 Alma Street Aston was in the centre of a row of terraced houses that fronted straight on to the street. The front parlour was for best and was therefore rarely used. The living room was divided from the parlour by an internal staircase that went up to two bedrooms and down to the coal cellar that was fed from a chute from the street. The small kitchen went out into the garden. Past that was the outside toilet. Built in Victorian times and council owned it was due for demolition, which would follow before too long.

What we loved best about Alma Street was the shop just a few doors along. The Piggotts had been there since just after the First World War and were well known. The shop owners were very friendly, and I simply loved the creamy Banana ice cream bars made by Midland Counties. Yum yum.

The only real downside was the smoking as they were both heavy smokers. However, they did pass on their collections of cigarette cards which I still have.

They were a quiet couple who did not laugh much but I think money was short and they had experienced a fairly tough life.

They didn't always get on and my Mom told me that my Grandad, who served on HMS Repulse in the first World War, re-joined the Navy at the outbreak of the second conflict even though he was over age. Apparently, this was to have a break from Grandma. He was found out and soon sent back to man anti-aircraft guns in local parks. My main memories of Grandad Piggott are sitting watching him enjoy his favourite sport on TV; boxing. He sat in his usual chair quietly puffing away on his Park Drive watching the blows landing.

Not so wizard in Oz

My Dad's sister Margaret (Auntie Marg), husband Charles (Uncle Charl) and their children, Peter and Christine, decided to experience life on the other side of the world and became £10 Poms. The deal enabled Brits to move to Australia for just £10 per adult (equivalent to over £400 in 2019) provided they stayed for at least two years.

Around one million Brits took part in the scheme between 1945 and 1972. Famous participants include Australian PM Julia Gillard, the Gibb brothers (The Bee Gees) and actor Hugh Jackman's parents.

Uncle Charl was a tool maker, a trade needed on the other side of the world as well as here in the UK. Off they went and settled in New South Wales. However, they were not happy. The main reasons were the hot weather and the insects. As soon as the two years were up, they were back living on the Coventry Road (A45) in another Dares three bedroom semi near to the Wagon and Horses pub not far from the Swan pub.

Now they were a family of five with the addition of baby Keith. I am not sure why, but we were never really close to them. Visits were rare but I don't think there was ever any falling out.

Cowboys and Indians

Like most youngsters at the time I was constantly playing cowboys and Indians, always wanting to be a cowboy as they seemed to have a much better deal according to the TV. The Lone Ranger had hit TV screens in the USA in 1949 but it came to the BBC screens on Christmas day 1956 at 16.50. Clayton Moore starred as the lone Ranger ably supported by Jay Silverheels as Tonto. I liked the way they always helped people in trouble and that no one knew who the masked man was.

This year saw the launch of a number of American westerns. Bonanza became my favourite due to the variety of its stories. It told the story of the wealthy Cartwright family headed by Ben played by Lorne Green. It was set in the 1860's on the huge Ponderosa ranch close to Lake Tahoe which I would visit some 43 years later. There were three brothers; Adam (played by Pernell Roberts), Hoss (Dan Blocker) and Little Joe (Michael Landon). Lorne Green was actually only 13 years older than the "sons" but he carried it off well. My favourite character was Hoss, a lovable giant with a ready smile. It was so popular it ran from 1959 ending in 1973 following Dan Blocker's death in 1972.

Keep them Doggies rolling

Rawhide gave actor Clint Eastwood his big break playing Rowdy Yates as the series launched this year. The weekly tale of drovers was also set in the 1860's with plenty of action.

Wagon Train, another series I grew to enjoy, also arrived. My favourite character was the comical cook Charlie B Wooster played by Frank McGrath. The wagon train travelled each week from Missouri to California and I loved to get on board. The train provided a great opportunity for guest appearances by the likes of Bette Davis, Ronald Reagan, Elizabeth Montgomery, John Wayne, James Caan and many more. Other westerns on TV at this time included Maverick starring James Garner and Gunsmoke starring Burt Reynolds.

Friends to die for

In my class at Hobmoor I had two friends who lived just around the corner. Peter Seeny lived at 21 Rockingham Road and Nigel Osgood lived at 4 Heathmere. They were regular cowboys or Indians and we all learned the art of being shot or arrowed to death and then falling dramatically to the ground. I had several toy guns and a very smart leather holster. No one seemed to worry about the implications of constant gun involvement, but I am pretty sure that none of my contemporaries have been adversely affected.

Sadly, both my pals were to leave the before too long. I don't know where Nigel went but Peter eventually left for Perth in Australia as the climate would help with his Dad's asthma. Just before Nigel left we stood in front of our class and sang "76 trombones" from the 1957 musical play "The Music Man". We received an appreciative round of applause, but it was clearly not enough to keep Nigel in town.

New friend

I lost two good friends but had gained another. John Lavender lived at 12 Rockingham Road, about 40 yards from me. His house backed on to Hobmoor Primary school by the sealed air raid shelters. John was in the year below me, but we had met through our Moms. There was a real plus as the Lavenders had ITV and I was delighted to be invited to view many different programmes. John and I are still good friends to this day.

Moving on up

As the schools restarted after the summer break, I expected to move up into Miss Trotter's class. I was shocked to learn that three of us would be moved up to the class above. It was very disappointing to leave almost all of my classmates behind.

I believe the move happened partly due to me being much older than most of the class and had already learnt to read before starting school. The odd thing is that all three of us stayed in class 3 for the following year. After the initial shock there was the benefit of making even more friends.

Other events in 1959

January 22 – British racing driver Mike Hawthorn killed when his Jaguar collides with a tree near Guildford

February 3 – Buddy Holly, Ritchie Valens and the Big Bopper die in a plane crash in the USA. Called "the day the music died"

February 23 – Prime Minister Macmillan meets Soviet leader Khruschev during visit to USSR (THIS IS A BIG 'SO WHAT!')
March 30 – 20,000 protesters attend a CND rally in Trafalgar square

April 22 – Ballerina Margo Fonteyn released from prison in Panama having been suspected of supporting a coup

May 2 – The Chapelcross nuclear power station opened in Scotland

June 1 – BBC launch Juke Box Jury chaired by David Jacobs. It ran until 1967

July 28 – First post codes launched in Norwich

August 26 – BMC (British Motor Corporation) launches the Mini with a top speed of 70mph. Designed by Alec Issigonis who had previously designed the Morris Minor
October 8 – Conservatives win third General Election with a majority of 100 seats. Margaret Thatcher wins Finchley

November – Ronnie Scott's jazz club opens

December – Car ownership exceeds 30% of home ownership

A great year for films with the release of; Ben Hur, Some like it Hot, North by North West and Sleeping Beauty

Best-selling UK single in 1959 Cliff Richard with Living Doll which spent 6 weeks at number 1

Chapter 4 1960: It's all at the Co-op

Divi up

With my Dad working for the Birmingham Co-op we were duty bound to shop there. Fortunately, the Co-op was our nearest shop being less than 200 yards away, just around the corner on Stoney lane. There were three shops in the building providing greengrocery, general grocery and a butcher.

The other incentive to shop there was the "divi". Every time you made a purchase you were asked for your dividend number and given a small receipt quoting that number and the amount spent. At the end of the year your account was given a dividend to spend in store. Everyone I knew had a six figure number but as an employee my Dad was able to pick his number from closed accounts hence an easy low number to remember; 2525. Whenever I gave our number I was greeted with "and the other two numbers please". I didn't find this annoying as I enjoyed being different, even special.

The wonder of "Woolies"

Woolworths was my favourite local shop at the Yew Tree. It was their 904th store and had opened on Church Road in about 1955. It was a great place for sweets as you could mix a variety of them together. It had a good selection of Airfix kits that I struggled to assemble without smearing glue in all the wrong places. Brother Steve, however, always made an excellent construction due to his superior patience and concentration. During regular visits with my Mom I would often spend a ridiculous amount of time playing with the cotton reels. They could be found at the far end of the store presented in neat lanes that they fitted perfectly. You could amuse yourself by pushing the reels back up each lane and watch them spin down the slight incline. What fun. Who needs video games?

Since Woolworths closed the building is now quite a smart Wetherspoons pub called the "William Tyler" named after the 15th century tiler. Yardley was once a busy centre for making tiles and home to 17 kilns at its peak in the 15th century. I still pay the occasional visit but "there ain't no cotton reels no more"!

Cold comfort

The lack of fridges meant that shopping was a far more regular task to ensure freshness. Supermarkets were yet to arrive, but the Yew Tree boasted a Masons, Wrensons and two or three small independent grocers.

Home deliveries were an important service. Again, the Co-op was dominant for both bread and milk deliveries. The breadman appeared from his wagon with his large wicker basket full of produce. I was always keen to encourage my Mom to add Wagon Wheels and cakes to her bread order. Only very occasionally was I successful. There were two other bread delivery services to the square; Hawleys and Hardings. The latter didn't have to travel far as the Hardings bakery was only a few minutes away at the top end of Church Road on the left hand side just before the Swan.

The Co-op milkman delivered quite early most days except for Friday and Saturday when his round included collecting payments. At weekends he would often have a young helper to speed up the round. There were three types of milk; standard pasteurised, Jersey (cream top) and sterilised. I have never been keen on drinking neat milk but could drink the sterilised variety, known as "stera", as long as it was cool. The Co-op had competition from Midland Counties but our house remained loyal to the Co-op and its "divi".

Not surprisingly the "pop man" was popular. Corona fizzy drinks were delivered by lorries to many homes across the country, but not ours. Steve and me were strictly rationed when it came to pop. I am not sure whether Mom was protecting our teeth, or her budget.

The other delivery in bottles declined by the Duffin household was Davenports beer promoted by advertisements pronouncing "beer at home means Davenports". Known mainly for its dark mild beers produced at their Highgate brewery close to the city centre. With my Dad a virtual teetotaller they were never likely to secure us as customers. The Betterwear man was a regular visitor. Selling brushes and other household goods such as polish. I always wanted to stand close to my mom and see what he was selling. I was often rewarded with a small gift such as a miniature tin of polish. Little things please little minds.

The lack of fridges was a real bonus to the ice cream man. His "ding dong" was heard not just in the summer as ice cream could not be kept without a fridge with a freezer compartment. Our favourite ice cream was a block of Neapolitan as perhaps a Sunday treat. In the summer months a more regular sight was the bike with a small fridge at the front with a sign saying "stop me and buy one", and we often did.

A real winner

Not delivering goods but providing a service was our window cleaner. He always wore a cap and smiled a lot even though you could count the number of his teeth on one or two fingers. He was our cleaner for many years although he did take unexpected early retirement. One day he announced excitedly that he had won the football pools and would no longer need to work.

Naturally my mom was pleased for him and wished him well. However, within a few months his barrow bearing his ladder and bucket reappeared. It was clear that he had not spent his winnings on new dentures and we never did find out what had happened, but he remained a regular visitor for many years.

Like many families we also did the football pools from time to time. The main providers were Littlewoods followed by Vernons and Zetters. We opted for the two smaller players presumably based on cost. When I later discovered radio Luxemburg, I also discovered Horace Batchelor who sold a system that he claimed would help you be successful with the football pools. He became known more for spelling out K E Y N S H A M when giving his postal address than helping people win.

The only regular visitor still using a horse was the rag and bone man. His cry of "any old iron" rang out from time to time and was a useful service as there were no recycling dumps and moving large items was difficult without a car. There was however some recycling of dumps as the horse's excrement found its way on to local gardens.

And so this is Christmas

Now aged seven I began to really understand the meaning of Christmas. It meant lots of fun at both school and home. At school we made chain decorations that required almost constant regluing but there was the school Christmas party to enjoy.

Fun and games were to be enjoyed after fish paste sandwiches and jelly in corrugated paper dishes were demolished. Homemade buns with tiny wings perched in the buttermilk filling were the centre of a boys' contest as to who could eat the most.

When the games started it was pass the parcel and musical chairs. This was when I found out how truly competitive I was, as I shoved a young girl out of my way to ensure a chance of grabbing first prize.

Heading to the Grotto

Mom took us up to town where the two best Grottos were to be found at the Co-op (of course) on High Street and Lewis's department store on Corporation Street. Steve and I both preferred Lewis's as it had the added attraction of Mr Holly and a whole floor of toys and Christmas goodies. We did make it there occasionally, but the downside was the long queues along the seemingly never-ending staircase. On the way into town on the number 17 bus, we would entertain ourselves on the three mile journey by counting the number of houses that had Christmas trees lit up in their front rooms.

TV times

There was great news as just before the big day Dad announced that a new television complete with ITV would arrive in time to catch all the festive fun. On the new channel we were able to watch our favourite, Robin Hood, at 6.30pm on Christmas Eve. We were then allowed to stay up to watch Sinbad the Sailor before bed at 9pm. On BBC we could watch the Lone Ranger at 5pm. There may have been some debate at 6.30 as Robin Hood clashed with Dixon of Dock Green, one of Mom's favourites. On Christmas Day afternoon the circus was always a favourite. Later there were variety shows such as Christmas Night with the Stars.

Going up the stairs to bed at an unusually late time on Christmas Eve did not help me go to sleep. Empty pillow cases were placed at the end of our beds and the excitement pulsed through my body. What would Santa bring, and would I see him?

He was not spotted and our "sacks" looked pretty full at 7am. Next to my "sack" was a pretty big parcel and I couldn't wait to tear the paper off to reveal the surprise. Our instructions were to wait to be invited into our parents' bedroom where we would dive into bed to open our presents.

Dad was sent to the freezing kitchen to make tea. My big parcel turned out to be a chuck wagon. This was just what I wanted as it fitted with my interest in the Wild West. It had every type of kitchen utensil you could think of. I was immediately playing "Cookie" from Wagon Train.

Grandpa and Nannah Duffin would arrive early morning followed by Mom's sister Aunt Joyce and her husband Uncle Cyril. Sherry and Snowballs were the drinks offered with lemonade for Steve and me. Mom prepared as much as she could in advance. She always made several Christmas puddings and mince pies a plenty for friends and relatives. Lunch was very traditional with plenty of lovely sprouts (well I like them), followed by Christmas pudding with custard and the hunt for the silver three pence piece that I was scared would choke me. Tea would be served late with the main feature being the Christmas iced fruit cake plus the compulsory wearing of hats from the crackers. Any TV lulls would be filled with card games such as "dirty windows" using matchsticks to record tricks won. Such happy memories.

Other events in 1960

February 18 – The Queen gives birth to a son, her third child

March – 20 year old footballer Dennis Law signs for Manchester City for a record fee of £55,000 from Huddersfield Town

April 17 – American rock singer Eddie Cochran (21) killed in a car crash in Wiltshire

May 6 – Princess Margaret marries photographer Anthony Armstrong-Jones in the first televised Royal wedding

July – The Shadows release the instrumental, Apache

August 17 – The Beatles appear in Hamburg

September 15 – First traffic wardens deployed in London

October 27 – The film Saturday Night and Sunday Morning released

November 10 – Lady Chatterley's Lover sells 200,000 copies in one day following its publication after being banned since 1928

December 9 – The first episode of the soap opera Coronation Street broadcast

Other.

The Grand National televised for the first time
The last man is called up for National Service, as Conscription ends
At the end of the year the Farthing coin ceased to be legal tender. It was first circulated in the 13th century
Bestselling UK single in 1960: "It's now or Never" by Elvis Presley

Chapter 5 1961: Summer holidays

New neighbours

There were developments afoot in Charminster Avenue. There was a new owner of the house opposite at number 8, one of the two new semis built on what was a small bomb site. The new owners were Birmingham City Football Club (aka the Blues) and their first tenant was the Blues centre half and Captain Trevor Smith.

I was already an Aston Villa fan as my Dad was a season ticket holder, but it was exciting to have such a well-known footballer just a few yards away, particularly as he had recently made his England debut. Trevor was a tall, powerfully built man but he was friendly and always said hello.

Allegiances questioned

One day Steve came running in to announce that Trevor had given him a complimentary ticket to the next Blues home game. There was a catch, really more of a quid pro quo. In return for the tickets Steve would keep Trevor's scrap book up to date. This was no problem for Steve as he loved that type of work and was already keeping a football scrap book of his own. What it did mean was that Steve would become a lifelong "Blue nose". Dad and I were just pleased that Steve was taking a keen interest in football even it was the wrong team. I was football mad and took a ball with me wherever I went.

Trevor played for the Blues at a time when they were quite successful. He appeared in the losing FA Cup Final in 1956 at the age of 20 and was on the losing side in two Inter City Fairs cup finals in both 1960 and 1961. His fortunes changed later when in 1963 he was on the winning side in the League Cup final against my Villa side.

Unfortunately, he developed arthritis and was sold to Walsall in 1964 for £18,000. He had to leave number 8 and load his scrap books in to the removal van. His arthritis flared up and he only managed 18 games for Walsall before retiring at just over thirty to run a pub in Tamworth.

When I look back, I find it hard to believe that a top professional footballer like Trevor lived in a rented semi across the road from us. How times have changed.

No longer fun at the YMCA

This year's summer holiday was a real change for the Duffins. Grandpa Duffin had been a member of the YMCA holiday centres for many years and my Dad carried on the family tradition. Although we didn't have a lot of spare cash, in fact probably none, we always managed to go on holiday for a week in the summer. The YMCA family holiday centres were reasonably priced and provided a much smaller and limited holiday camp atmosphere. No red or blue coats, just duffle coats when the weather turned. Three meals a day were provided together with fairly basic accommodation. There was usually a snooker table and table tennis. Activities were provided for children including a fancy-dress competition.

Gavin and Stacey yet to appear

There were a small number of YMCA holiday centres across the country, but our favourite was situated on the Knap at Barry in South Wales. Close to Cardiff allowing relatively straight forward rail travel it was also near to Barry Island with its fine sandy beach, funfair and other tourist attractions. We had been to Barry three times in the last four years. The exception was the YMCA in Rhyl in 1958 where Steve and I had won first prize in the children's fancy dress competition dressed as a zebra crossing.

It was a pebble beach at Barry and we liked to move the pebbles to create bunkers providing shelter from any stiff breeze. The sandy beach at Barry Island was ideal for digging roads for our dinky cars and burying each other. Trenches were built to temporality stop the tide destroying our handy work. Small flags were purchased to sit proudly on top of our sandcastles. One of our favourite haunts was the Forte café where many chocolate milk shakes with floating ice cream were eagerly consumed. It was here that I discovered a lifelong aversion to Coca-Cola. I am sorry I just don't like the taste!

Butlins by the sea

One of the downsides of our recent access to ITV was the exposure to powerful advertising. Butlins were regularly advertising their attractive Holiday camps which seemed to have everything a family could wish for. Steve and I were sold on the funfairs and swimming pools. So much to do and it was all free! My Dad was less impressed as it certainly wasn't free for him, and a lot of the entertainment was focused around the bars. Nevertheless, we were delighted when Dad announced that he had booked a holiday at Butlins.

Clacton here we come

There were several Butlins camps to choose from. I am not sure why he chose Clacton on Sea but as we did not have a car a railway station was a must. As on all our previous holidays we packed a large case and sent it in advance by rail to lighten our load. We covered the case in hessian and Mom sowed it up tight for protection and security.

A perk of my Dad's job was access to the Daimler cars used by the funeral section and to ferry the directors around. A chauffeur driven car would collect us and drop us off at the station in town.

I was always so excited by this. It felt as though we were really posh and it was a great way to start our holidays. Steam trains were still common with separate carriages and long corridors. Stickers instructing you not to put your head out of the window were strategically placed and well observed for obvious reasons. I loved travelling by train and still do.

Steve and I had a great time at Butlins, helped by good weather. In and out of the pools and enjoying the almost constant entertainment supported by the enthusiastic team of Redcoats. Famous Redcoats include Des O'Connor and Jimmy Tarbuck, but I don't think either were at Clacton at the time. My Dad's fears regarding the focus on alcohol were proven right and a return to the YM looked almost certain.

Turning a blind eye

In September I joined class 4 under Mrs Miller. Almost straight away we were told that we would be having an eye test. We were put in groups and waited to be called into the room. When it was my turn I sat calmly and as instructed I read out the numbers I could see amongst the coloured dots. I passed the test with flying colours.

I was then asked to read the chart on the wall with my left eye. My right eye being covered up. No problem with that either. Then the shock came. The nurse covered my left eye and asked me to read the chart. I was stunned as I could not read anything. Not even the top letter. I burst into tears. I didn't know what to do. The nurse told me they would contact my parents and not to worry as there were things that could be done to improve my sight. I was in a state of shock and it took some time for me to be calm enough to return to my class.

Patched up

Birmingham and Midland Eye Hospital was situated in Church Street in the city centre. Mom and I started a regular trip to see Mr M J Roper-Hall or one of his many assistants.

The problem was quickly identified. I had a squint in my right eye which had prevented my vision to fully develop.
I had a lazy eye where my brain had switched off the signals to my right eye due to poor reception. Our vision develops for the first seven years of our lives. I had just had my eight birthday which meant we were a little late in trying to correct the problem.

There were two treatment options to rectify the squint; surgery or eye exercise by covering my good eye. I was on the borderline so it was decided to start with exercise and if that didn't work, we would move to surgery. We started off putting a patch over my good left eye to make my right eye work harder and come in line. It was pretty traumatic at first as I could not see anything like I could before. At school I was moved to the very front of the class but I still had to remove my patch when reading. The good news was that my classmates were very sympathetic and for a while I was the centre of attention. I was instructed to wear the patch for 4 to 6 hours per day. I was keen to follow this as I really wanted my vision to improve.

The regular trips to the eye hospital continued but I was making good progress. The equipment used to measure the squint was fun. I had to rest my chin with each eye looking into an eye piece. The left eye could see a rabbit and the right eye focused on a carrot. By moving a metal handle on each side, I had to put the carrot in the rabbit's hand. There were other cartoons with a similar scene.

After a few months of wearing patches it was decided that the progress I was making made surgery unnecessary. I was delighted and had become accustomed to wearing a patch. There were occasional disputes such as pleading for removal when going to see the circus, but I came through it smiling at knowing it was working.

Progress was slow but my vision improved, and I moved to wearing glasses with the lens in front of the good left eye covered in nail varnish to block my vision. I can still smell it. Eventually the squint was declared cured with my vision improved but nowhere near as good as it would have been without the squint.

Other UK events in 1961

January – Bingo Halls made legal. Betting shops followed in May

January 20 – John F Kennedy sworn in as 35th President of the USA

February 8 – Beatles perform at the Cavern Club for the first time

March 13 – The black and white five pound note ceases to be legal tender

April 12 – Soviet cosmonaut Yuri Gagarin becomes the first human in space orbiting the earth once. Six weeks later American president announces the Apollo programme aiming to put a man on the Moon before the end of the decade

May 14 – USA civil rights movement freedom riders' bus is fire bombed and protesters beaten by Ku Klux Klan members

August 10 – UK applies for membership of EEC (European Economic Community)

August 13 – Construction of the Berlin Wall begins

September 1 – First Mothercare store opens

October 25 – The satirical magazine Private Eye published

November 10 – Catch 22 by Joseph Heller published

Other

At the end of the year birth control pills became available on the NHS

Barbie doll gets a boyfriend when Ken arrives

TV saw the arrival of the Avengers starring Honor Blackman and Patrick Macnee and Gerry Anderson's Supercar travelling on land sea and air

Best-selling UK single in 1961 "Wooden Heart" by Elvis Presley. From the film G I Blues it stayed at number for 6 weeks

Chapter 6 1962: Football Fever

Up the Villa

I think it was seeing my brother Steve going down to watch the Blues, courtesy of free tickets from their captain Trevor Smith, that encouraged me to make my first trip to Villa Park. With my friend Peter Seeney having his bags packed for his move to Australia, we just had time for my Dad to accompany us on the number 11 (Outer Circle bus) to the hallowed turf for our first ever game. It was Easter Monday with a 3pm kick off. We were so excited.

My Dad had a season ticket for a seat in the Witton Lane stand. He took Peter and I to the gate for the open standing area at the Witton Lane end (Gate K). He paid the man at the turnstile and gave us clear instructions to wait for him at the same spot when the match finished. Due to our restricted height we made our way down to the very front to one side of the goal to allow a reasonable view even at pitch level.

I couldn't have chosen a better match to start my lifelong support. We were 4-1 up by half time and finished comfortably beating Nottingham Forest 5-1. There were two goals for popular Villa winger Harry Burrows. Unfortunately, there were no goals from centre forward Derek Dougan, signed for £15k at the start of the season. The "Doog" was brought in to replace prolific scorer Gerry Hitchens (96 goals in 160 games) who had been sold at the end of the previous season to the Italian club Inter Milan for a staggering British record of £85k.

When the final whistle blew Dad was there to meet us as planned and we smiled all the way home, despite waiting a long while in the queue near Witton railway station for our bus home.

I don't think many eight year olds would be left without adult supervision these days, just one of the many things that have changed in football.

Salaries were a tiny fraction of today's almost obscene level for top players. The money pumped into the game by television has led to a distorted sport. Gone are the days where many of the players were recruited locally and lived modestly like our neighbour Trevor Smith. The standard of the football has improved but at what cost?

Funny tasting coffee

My friend Peter went down under the next week. However, I returned to see the Villa with Dad taking me into the stand by slipping the turnstile attendant a few bob and lifting me over the turnstile. The stand usually had spare seats, but I had to sit on his knee when it was full. Dad sat with three of our close neighbours; Cissie Eccles (yes, the one who stopped everyone to chat at her gate), her sister Reenie Holliday and her husband Chris, who all lived at number 3 Charminster. At half time Reenie would bring out a flask of the strangest tasting coffee. It would be several years before I realised it was laced with whisky. I never commented on the unusual taste as it was very welcome particularly in the winter.

On the trolley

That summer the sun brought out many other children around the square and a craze started. I am not sure who was responsible for building the first trolley. It may have been Keith Jinks from Rockingham Road or Alan Horton from the top of Heathmere Avenue. After a homemade trolley appeared another soon followed. Both Alan and Keith were a year or two older than me and were very practical. Homemade trollies or Karts started to appear everywhere.

Steve was keen for us to build one which meant it would be down to him of course. The rear wheels came from our old pram that had been stored in the garage since I last climbed out several years previously. The front wheels were from an old scooter.

The seat was recovered from an old chair and re-upholstered with material from a discarded black plastic "pac-a-mac" providing a waterproof covering. The finishing touch was a lino covering on the exposed wooden area. Steve spent time meticulously preparing it for its first run and it looked great. I was hardly involved in the construction, but my excitement was building as it took shape.

The one drawback affecting the trollies was the lack of propulsion as they all had to rely on being pushed. Half a dozen trollies set off on the first round the square race with me clutching the rope to steer the front wheels. Steve pushed as fast as he could, but we failed to lead partly due to my total inexperience. If there had been a prize for the best looking kart, we would surely have won it. Our concentration on looks had led to a weight problem that was not suffered by our rivals. It was still great fun but there was a frightening moment when momentum was built on the downhill Rockingham Road. As went around the corner into Charminster only two of the four wheels were in contact with the pavement. It was a passing phase with most of the enjoyment coming from creating the trollies rather than using them.

No Butlins

Given Dad's reaction to the focus on the bars at Butlins last summer it was no surprise that we were heading to a YMCA family centre for our summer holiday. Steve and I had had fun at Butlins the previous year, however Dad was determined to head down to a YMCA we had not been to before in Eastbourne on the south coast. Victoria Court was in a prime position on Grand Parade overlooking the sandy beach.

We were there for a week from Saturday 11th August in room 19, a family room overlooking the sea. It was more of a formal hotel than the other YM centres. It did have table tennis and snooker in the basement. Mum and Dad loved the south coast, in particular genteel Eastbourne with its bandstand and numerous deck chairs all lined up to face the sun and music.

There was less to entertain us boys. We did pay one shilling to play on the putting green. Unfortunately, I thought I was Arnold Palmer and struck dad in the face with a completely over the top backswing. He was pretty good about the blow and having to wear a plaster all week. On the Wednesday evening we went to the Pier Theatre where popular comedian Tommy Comedian Tommy Trinder topped the bill (catch phrase "you lucky people"). His rather risqué rendition of "Susie, Susie sitting in the shoeshine shop" had me in stiches as I knew exactly what he meant. It still comes back to me on occasions.

Also on the bill was another old time comedian, Sandy Powell, known for his catch phrase "can you hear me mother". He was a regular performer at the Pier Theatre for many years during the 50's and early 60's but he didn't make me smile like TT.

Like most holiday makers, the ritual of sending postcards back home to friends and relatives was observed. My role was to help Mom choose the best cards that were on sale along the front. They had to be sent early in the week to avoid the cards arriving after we had returned home. The YMCA had its own cards picturing the front of the hotel. I marked the card to identify our rooms. There was always a comment on the weather, and I think Tommy Trinder received a mention. Apart from relatives we always sent cards to our close neighbours who would do the same when they were away.

We set back home on the steam train after an enjoyable holiday and I knew Mom and Dad had enjoyed it so much we would soon be back.

Ill again

Like most kids of my age I went through most of the childhood illnesses. Measles, Mumps, Chicken pox, German measles, Scarlet fever, you name it I had it. There wasn't an MMR vaccine (measles, mumps and rubella aka German measles) but there was an effective vaccine against polio from 1955.

When it was time for my polio booster, I was dreading the needle but there was good news as my very last polio vaccine was delivered on a sugar cube. How sweet was that?

We were registered with Dr Donavon and partners at the surgery near the Swan in Willard Road next to the Oaklands playing fields. You couldn't make appointments you just had to sit in the waiting room and shuffle up towards the doctor's door as each patient vacated the consulting room clutching a prescription. There was a prescription charge of two shillings (10p) which was waived for children under 16.

The doctor would also make home visits if you were too ill to make it to the surgery. I frequently suffered tonsillitis (inflammation of the tonsils). I had it so often the doctor usually said, "If he has it again we'll take them out". I did, but they didn't! It usually cleared up in a few days but occasionally I was so ill that I had a very high temperature and suffered hallucinations. The problem continued into adulthood with the last episode occurring whilst following the England cricket team in India in 2006 (the full story can be found in my book "The Cricket Was Good Too" available on Amazon with all royalties to Sense the deafblind charity).

"Oi'll give it foive"

It may have been linked with it being close to my ninth birthday, and I am not sure how Dad managed to secure the tickets but in September Dad, Steve and I were off to the Alpha television studios in Aston to watch the recording of "Thank Your Lucky Stars" (TYLS). The studios had originally been the home of the Theatre Royal Aston. In 1927 it turned into the Astoria cinema before its transformation into the Alpha television studios in 1956.

Thank Your Lucky Stars was a pop music show made by ABC television and broadcast on ITV. It featured many of the top pop groups including The Beatles and The Rolling Stones.

My favourite on our visit were the Tornadoes with the instrumental Telstar. It reached number one both here and in the States. It was written and produced by Joe Meek and it was probably no coincidence that he also produced Billy Fury who appeared on the same show. It was so exciting as a nine-year-old to see these stars. I think it set me off on the road to loving music and watching live performances even if these early ones were mimed.

The show had several presenters including Brian Matthew and Keith Fordyce. Our show was presented by Pete Murray. There was an interesting section called "spin a disc" where DJ Alan Freeman played three records to be judged by a panel of three teenagers giving a rating between one and five. This is where local office girl Janice Nichols made a name for herself with her catch phrase "Oi'll give it foive" pronounced in her strong black country accent.

The programme began in 1961 with over 2000 acts appearing on the show. It predated the BBC's Top of the Pops which started in 1964. However, TYLS suffered from the competition and only lasted another year.

School, on a Sunday?

I was enjoying school and was now under a really inspirational teacher. Class 5 was led by Miss Wright. Okay she obviously enjoyed more than a crafty fag as evidenced by two yellow stained fingers on her right hand and the smell of smoke on her clothes, but she made everything interesting. I loved the time she spent reading to us, particularly the book "Heidi".

I must have enjoyed school so much that I did not object when Steve and I were taken to Sunday school by our next-door neighbours the Beresfords. We shared a drive with them, and Dad Eric Beresford drove a Vauxhall at the time.

Trips in a car were a rare treat which may have been part of the initial attraction. Their daughter Joy was about a year younger than Steve and the three of us were driven to the Gospel Hall on Waterloo Road not far from the Swan at the far end of Graham Road. My first teacher was the lovely Miss Ross. The atmosphere was very relaxed, and I was taken with the regular gift of stickers. I have always been a "joiner" and I liked being part of another group. I turned up regularly and that year I was awarded a third prize for regular attendance.

The Beresford family were firmly established at what we called "The Hall" along with some of their other relatives notably the Yardley's. Steve and I continued to attend for many years as it became an extended family. I am sure the grounding helped form my moral compass along with making some very good friendships.

UK Events in 1962

January 2 – 'Z Cars' launched by BBC

February 4 – Sunday Times launches first colour supplement

March 6 – Accrington Stanley leave the football league due to huge debts

April 6 - Panda crossings introduced (later became Pelican crossings)

May 25 – New Coventry Cathedral consecrated

June 14 – BBC launch Steptoe and Son

July 11 – First Live TV broadcast from USA via Telstar

August 17 – The Tornados record the hit single Telstar

September 8/11 – Last ever Gentlemen v Players cricket match takes place at Scarborough

October 5 – 'Dr No' the first Bond film premiers in London.
First Beatles single "Love me do" released by Parlophone

November 29 – Britain and France agree to develop Concorde

December 10 – David Lean's 'Lawrence of Arabia' released

Big freeze begins on 22nd December with no frost free nights until March 5th 1963

Best-selling single in 1962: Frank Ifield" I Remember You", selling 1.1 million and staying seven weeks at Number 1.

Chapter 7 1963:   In the swim

Winter draws on

Boy it was cold! The freeze affected everything. Even the sea froze off Herne Bay in Kent. Sport was badly affected with football matches continually having to be rescheduled as under pitch heating was yet to be introduced. The FA Cup was delayed, and the season was extended by four weeks. The "Pools Panel" sat regularly to give their view of the outcome of postponed matches to enable the football pools to continue.

Although not aware of it at the time, even burying the dead became difficult as spades bounced off the frozen surface. In the main, schools adjusted and remained open. We pulled our socks up as high as possible as we all wore short trousers up until starting big school at age 11. We did have some fun though as the steps in our back garden became a snow covered slope for several weeks which Steve and I slid down on a piece of metal about three feet square. We spent hours getting soaked through trying unsuccessfully to build an igloo.

The thaw eventually came in March and life quickly returned to normal. However, it took the lawn in our back garden a lot longer to recover after the bashing we had given it.

The flicks

The nearest cinema had been the Tivoli on the Coventry Road near the Swan but it closed in the summer of 1961. This left the Adelphi further down the Coventry Road towards the city centre in Hay Mills, and the Beaufort in Ward End, both a bus ride away. Steve and I had been to a couple of Saturday morning viewings at the Adelphi courtesy of Butlins due to our membership of the "Beaver Club" (motto: Be as eager as a beaver) for 2 to 8 year olds and Club 913 for ages 9 to 14.

Following our visit to Butlins Clacton in 1961 we had received the invitations once a year which gave free entry plus two tear off strips for a free ice cream and cold drink. This was all part of Butlins' ploy to encourage us to put pressure on our parents to return to Butlins.

During the school holidays Mum took Steve and I to the Adelphi to see two completely different films. The first was "Hercules Unchained". It was made in 1959 but did the rounds regularly when cinemas needed to fill an empty space. It was a treat to go to the cinema, but the ice cream was probably the highlight. Next was a much more enjoyable viewing as we boarded the bus with Cliff Richard to venture on a "Summer Holiday". It was a jolly affair with other memorable tunes including "Batchelor Boy" and The Shadows playing "Foot Tapper". It was such a treat to see the big screen and in glorious technicolour.

YMCA Barry, again!

This was my fourth visit to YMCA at the Knap in Barry south Wales. Dad had decided to return as some modernisation had taken place with en-suite facilities added to a small number of bedrooms (not the boys' room though). The weather was really good, in fact so good that Dad ventured into the sea which was indeed a rarity.

As well as football I was cricket mad and the West Indies were touring with the formidable fast bowling pair Wes Hall and Charlie Griffiths tormenting the English batsman. Even my favourite player and England's captain Ted Dexter found life difficult that summer. Steve and I carefully rearranged the pebbles on the stony nearby beach to create a private hollow and sat glued to dad's transistor radio listening to the test match. We lost the series 3-1 but the cricket was entertaining.

Splashing out in Stechford

There was great local excitement towards the end of June as a new swimming baths opened in Stechford just four stops along the Outer Circle bus route. It had two pools, a beginners' pool and a full-size main pool complete with diving boards. These were set at three levels including a springboard at the second level. I was nearly ten years old but had not yet learnt to swim. This was my chance. Joy from next door was about two years older than me and a good swimmer. During the main school holidays Steve, Joy and I went to Stechford several times and with Joy's help I began to make progress.

Steve developed a unique swimming style that was somewhere between a whale and a frog. I was keen to be able to swim before moving to senior school in a year's time where swimming would form part of the curriculum for the first couple of years. I managed to make my first successful strokes thanks to Joy and Steve's support. They literally held me up at first and I gradually progressed. It would be some time before I progressed to diving of the side let alone the diving boards. After getting changed we would run upstairs to the café which overlooked the pools.

The complex was so popular that sessions were introduced and defined by coloured wrist bands. At first you could leave your clothes in the individual changing cubicles. This was soon replaced by baskets which you handed over in exchange for your wrist band. My visits also meant new trunks to replace the woollen ones that held some much water there was a constant battle to keep them up.

Out and about with Aunty Joyce

Mum's sister, Aunty Joyce married Cyril Potter when she was thirty and he was fifty. This did not go down too well at first with my grandparents as they thought the age difference would be a problem.

This led to them not attending their wedding in 1954. Aunt Joyce never spoke about her parents' initial reaction, fortunately her Mom and Dad came round and grew to be fond of Cyril.

They had planned to start a family but unfortunately it wasn't to be. However, Steve and I received much love and support from the Potters and probably became partial substitutes for their own lack of children. During the long school Summer Holiday, we enjoyed many trips with Mom and Aunty Joyce.

Son of a gun

Our first trip that summer was to Dudley Castle. This was familiar territory for Mom and Joyce as they had grown up in Aston which was not far away. Their parents, John and Emma Piggott, were from West Bromwich which is even closer to Dudley. I still have pictures of different generations sitting on the large cannons and we were soon continuing the family tradition. The castle dates back to c1070 but was in ruins. It housed a zoo, but our biggest thrill was sitting on the chair lift whilst eating an ice cream.

Keepers Pool

On the same side of town but over to the east was Sutton Park, also a regular attraction for the sisters when they were young. The huge park is one of the largest urban parks in Europe boasting 2400 acres.
Aunty Joyce insisted that Steve and I followed another family tradition and strip off and dip into "Keepers Pool". It was originally a fish pool and not designed for swimming. It was absolutely freezing despite the blazing sun and Steve and I escaped as quickly as we could having met our Aunt's demands. As soon as we were dry and clothed, we slowly made our way to the café in search of, yes, more ice cream.

Cutle Meadow

Joyce and Cyril lived in a three bedroomed semi very similar to ours but probably fifteen years newer. It was situated on the busy Chester Road at Bacons End, close to the overspill housing estate at Kingshurst. They had lived there since they were married in 1954. My grandparents John and Emma Piggott were moved out of their old Victorian terraced house in 1962 as a new road was being built in Aston leading to their home in Alma Street being demolished. They had moved into a brand new council bungalow in Kingshurst, just a short walk from Joyce and Cyril. Cyril was now fully accepted and the Piggotts were very pleased to move into a modern bungalow close to their daughter. It also meant that we saw a little bit more of my grandparents but they remained a quiet and introspective couple.

On the opposite side of the Chester Road were open fields. It provided not only a lovely view but a very pleasant area in which to stroll. The route to Joyce's meant a change of buses at the Fox and Goose, moving from the Birmingham Corporation Outer Circle to the Midland Red. The Midland Red bus always seemed a bit posher than the Birmingham Corporation equivalent. Maybe it was the folding rear door or just the better seat covers. Or perhaps it was the tickets that were printed on better paper and reminded me of the ones we were given when on holiday.

I remember the sun shining and after meeting up with Joyce we crossed the little service road before carefully making our way across the busy main road. On entering Cutle Meadow we were soon chasing butterflies and running aimlessly. I was not allowed to bring a football with me which was like losing my right arm or nowadays one's mobile phone. Further on there was a stream and Steve and I spent ages looking for newts, frogs and sticklebacks, without much success. Our picnic was lovely but sadly there was no ice cream.

'OO' it's Typhoo

Back at Joyce's she gave me a bag full of small pictures of football teams cut from Typhoo tea packets. When you had 12 pictures you could post them to Typhoo Tea for a 10" x 8" colour team photo of your choice from the range of 24 different teams. The cut outs came from one of Joyce's neighbours who in turn brought them back from where they worked, and a lot of tea must have been consumed. This went on for several years and I managed to complete several series of 24 colour photos of teams and later individual players too. I am an unashamed horder and still have them all, although the Aston Villa ones are a bit worse for wear having been constantly displayed. I was lucky and grateful that Steve was not interested in sharing the spoils.

The games people play

The Hobmoor school playground was surrounded by school buildings on three sides and a row of sealed air raid shelters on the remaining side. The playground was home to our varying attempts to organise and enjoy a range of games and activities during break time. My favourite was Hot Rice also known as Tig Ball. It was like touch tig except a tennis ball was used to 'tig' people. The person who was "on" to throw the ball was chosen by all the participants standing in a circle with feet apart and arms linked. The ball was then dropped in the middle and if the ball ran through your legs you were "on" and had to throw the ball and hit someone to join you.

The other main action game was British Bulldog. We all stood against the wall below the main hall and had to run to the other side without being touched by the "guards".

For those of a quieter disposition there was marbles played just in front of the old air raid shelters. Setting foot on the shelters themselves was strictly forbidden as I found out to my cost one day.

I was always curious to find out if they were actually full of water as we had often been warned. I was caught investigating the rear of one of the shelters by a teacher on playground duty. The backs of my legs were sore for a few days after they had been whacked with a ruler. I am not sure if the shelters were ever used by pupils during the war but a couple of bombs did fall in the school grounds during the night of the 22nd of November 1940. Fortunately no damage was recorded (to be found in an excellent book called "Raiders Past; Air raids on Yardley" by John V Abbott ISBN 1 85858 019 6).

Another gentle game was the old favourite; Hopscotch, which needed chalk to mark out the squares on which your stone would have to land. Most of the games were favoured by the boys, however, as time went on I discovered Kiss Chase but found myself being very selective i.e Susan Ball.

In the autumn the playground could become a little dangerous as conkers were flying everywhere. Different treatments were applied to make them as hard as possible from baking in the oven to soaking in vinegar. When they were ready for action a hole had to be made through the centre for a length of string to be added. When battle commenced it was all good clean fun except when the accuracy was a little lacking and the hardened "beast" struck your hand rather than the other little "beast".

Break time also saw us queue up in Mrs Roberts's room (the school secretary) for tuck. My favourites were chocolate whirlygigs but I also liked jammy dodgers and those pink wafers. We were also able to queue to buy national savings stamps. I was of course exempt from this due to lack of funds.

I used to go home for lunch, so I missed the fun of school dinners. My friend Peter Barker who lived opposite the school entrance recalls being ambushed by someone's dropped swede, which led to him slipping over, and dropping a whole jug of custard plus several plates in view of everyone including the hawk eyed and very strict Mrs Wilcox.

The school hall was also used for PE and country dancing. The latter was not particularly popular, and I remember the girls dreading having to hold hands with one poor lad who was covered in warts. We nearly all suffered warts at some stage but this lad was unfortunately covered from head to foot.

Kick off

In September I entered class 6 with Mr Hughes in charge. He was one of only two male teachers, the other being Mr Brookes (Aka Brooksy). Mr Hughes was responsible for boys' sport including selecting football and cricket teams. As we were a small school it was relatively easy to be selected as there were so few of us to choose from. During the summer I had made one appearance in the cricket team due mainly to my Dad's coaching and the lack of interest from some of the boys in the sound of leather on willow.

I made my way into the football team accepting any position as long as I got a game. We nearly always lost but despite our numerous defeats I was full of enthusiasm. Each week we would be marched across the road and up Hobmoor Croft on to the Oaklands for practice. This was the start of my passion for both sports despite my obvious disadvantage of restricted vision.

Other events in 1963

January- Worst winter since 1946/47

January 11- The film Summer Holiday starring Cliff Richard premieres in London

January 29- French President Charles de Gaulle vetoes UK entry into EEC

February 14- Labour party elect Harold Wilson as leader

March 22- Beatles release debut album Please Please Me

March 27- Beeching report issued calling for huge cuts to the rail network

May 2- The Beatles first number one single From Me to You

May 13- National Service ends as last service men released

June 5- Profumo affair breaks

August 8- The Great Train Robbery rakes place at Ledburn

September 1- Sindy doll marketed

September 12- Beatles second number one with She Loves You

September 26- Vauxhall Viva launched

November 22- President Kennedy assassinated in Dallas, Texas

November 23- First episode of Dr Who

December 12- Beatles third number one single of the year I Want to Hold Your Hand

Also:

The Lava lamp launched

Best-selling single in 1963 the Beatles, She Loves You remained in the UK charts for 31 consecutive weeks

Dad, Mum and me on holiday in Barry

Shops on corner of Church Rd and Croft rd at the Yew Tree, Woolworths on the extreme right

9 Charminster Avenue Duffin's residence

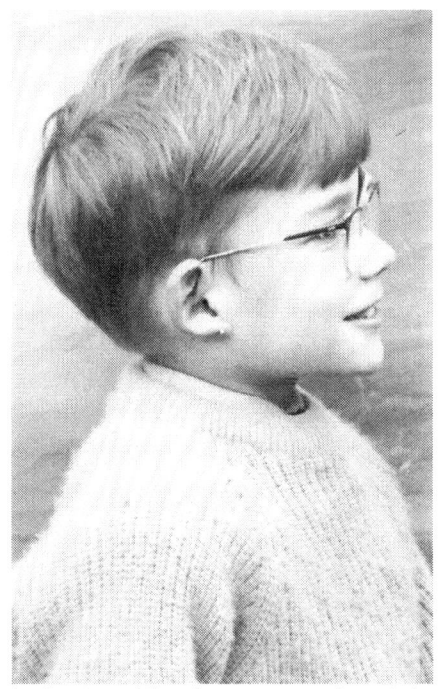

School photo with glasses and patch c1962

Rare evidence of Dad venturing into the sea

The Yew Tree pub c1960 well before Rio Grande added

Chapter 8 1964:   A player arrives

Twisting Dad's arm

Just before the end of the previous year someone brought the Beatles hit single "She Loves You" to the school Christmas party and at just ten years of age I became a firm Beatles fan. So much so that in March I went to Woolworths at the Yew Tree and parted with 6/8 (about 33p) to purchase their next single "Can't Buy Me Love". There was a slight problem as we did not own a record player. I thought my Dad would accuse me of wasting my money but to my huge relief and delight he told me he would look for a second hand record player.

Within a couple of weeks, he brought one home. He had bought it from someone at work. It was not exactly state of the art, but it worked, and I was delighted as was brother Steve. Steve bought The Animals "House of The Rising Sun" and we treated Mum to Cilla Black's "You're My World". Later in the year when Dad became ill, we bought the Beatles "I Feel Fine" to cheer him up, there was of course a little bit of self-interest.

My first EP (extended play) soon followed. I think I paid 10/6 (52p) for 'The Beatles Hits' from the record shop on the left-hand side of Church Road just before the Swan.
The four tracks were; From Me to You, Thank You Girl, Please Please Me and Love Me Do. EP's Usually had about four tracks with two on each side.

"A Hard Day's Night"

During the summer holidays Mom and Dad took us to see the first Beatles film "A Hard Day's Night' at the Odeon in New Street. We loved the whole experience especially the music. A few weeks later I was overjoyed to receive my first long playing (LP) record of the soundtrack of the film, it cost 32/- (£1.60) and ran about three times the length of an EP.

I played it continually driving everyone mad. It has since amused me to think of Steptoe and Son's Wilfred Brambell starring in the Beatles film, but I am not sure I made the connection at the time.

In Steptoe, Bramwell played the irascible father often referred to by his son as "you dirty old man". He played a very different role in the film as Paul McCartney's dapper, well-spoken grandfather. His character was constantly referred to as that "clean old man" making a humorous contrast to his more well-known role in Steptoe and Son.

Rock on Tommy

My friend John Lavender who lived close by at number 12 Rockingham Road had a pet guinea pig called Georgie. Not long after bringing it home she gave birth and a new home was needed for the male offspring. My Mom and Dad were not too keen at first but after I promised to clean it out regularly "Tommy" settled in to 9 Charminster. Dad made the hutch from wooden boxes with two sections. The left side had wire mesh and the right-hand side was his closed sleeping quarters. He squeaked often and did little else apart from his "business" of which there was more than enough. In the summer we made him a secure "run" in the garden and he seemed to enjoy his freedom. I did keep my promise to clean his cage but Tommy gave very little in return. With hindsight the decision to accept Tommy was a little rash and one I was careful not to repeat.

The only other pets up to this point were a couple of mice I brought home that soon became too many mice and had to be released in the garden. There was also an annual intake of frogspawn from the pond close to the nearby cricket field. We kept them in an old sink outside until they became frogs and hopped off to pastures new.

Dib dib

I am not sure who first encouraged me to join the Cubs but it turned out to be a good experience. I was a member of 261 A pack St Edburgha's. We met at the back of 150 Yardley Fields Road, Yardley which was about a twenty-minute walk from my house. My friend John Lavender was also in the same pack and his Dad would usually take us there in his car. Also in my pack were Rodney Wood and Steve Clayton who both lived on Heathmere Avenue. Rodney was in my class at Hobmoor but Steve went to Church Road primary school.

I enjoyed my time in the Cubs under our friendly and effective Akela June Dadd. The camaraderie was excellent, and I even did as I was told by my "sixer" despite him often being a bit too keen to give his orders. The highlight of the year was a camping weekend in York's Wood not far from Aunty Joyce and Uncle Cyril. There wasn't much sleep for any of us as it poured with rain both nights. We kept ourselves entertained telling jokes and making signs using our torches. There was much hilarity in the tent mostly due to an array of unclaimed sounds and smells. There were lots of other packs at the camp site and meals were a series of long queues, but it was great fun during the sunny day time with many games and challenges.

Away from camp I liked to design and make things and decided to enter the Yardley Cubs Handicraft Competition held at Garratts Green Technical College. My plasticine music man, complete with technicoloured guitar won an award certificate which, as a hoarder, I still have.

When it came time to move up the scouts the following year, I lasted two sessions. I didn't like the far more serious approach. The fun had gone and I missed the friends I had left behind, even my bossy "sixer".

Do you eat the red ones last?

I loved Rowntrees' Smarties and looked forward to Saturday morning when Mom would produce a box of the sugar-coated chocolates to be shared with Steve. We would tip the contents out on to the dining room table and begin to divide the contents. One of us would claim the box and the other would have the bag to store their share.

I am not sure if it was due to the advertising strapline used in the 1960's; "do you eat the red ones last", but I always wanted the stronger colours such as brown, orange and of course red. Fortunately Steve was completely relaxed and not at all colour prejudiced.

Toothpaste in a tin

Looking back, I did consume a lot of sweets and biscuits. We seem to have a regular supply of Nice, Malted Milk and Sportsman's biscuits which I often munched lubricated with orange cordial.

The only protection my teeth received came out of a tin. Gibbs pink toothpaste had to be scraped out of the round tin. It did not offer much protection as my frequent visits to Harvey Road clinic proved. I can remember only too well the smell of the gas and the strange unworldly feeling as I came round after tooth extraction. Rubbish toothpaste and no fluoride (and too many sweet things).

We suffered much more tooth decay than the current generation who fare much better due mainly to fluoride in our water and better dental care. However, there was very little obesity probably due to lack of both money and junk food.

Welcome to Warner's

Surprisingly Dad chose Warner's Minster holiday camp on the Isle of Sheppey for our summer holiday. He was clearly trying to please us as it had more to offer for children than a YMCA but fell short of the wide range of attractions at the probably more expensive Butlins. Steve and I enjoyed the pool and the entertainment. I am not sure our parents had such a good time. I feared a return to the YM next year.

Sent to Coventry

In the last week before the long summer break there was an organised school trip. We were sent to Coventry to visit the new cathedral which had been open for about two years. We also explored the ruins of the old cathedral which was bombed in the Second World War. Coventry suffered many bombing raids during the war due to its manufacturing capability, with the most destructive raid taking place on November 14th 1940. Over 500 German bombers took part in the devastating raid. Nearly 600 people were killed and more than 4300 homes destroyed. The cathedral was hit many times and was eventually destroyed.

The new cathedral was designed by Sir Basil Spence and took six years to build. Its modern design caused much comment particularly amongst local people, but it was soon accepted. It wasn't the most inspiring day out but better than being sat behind a desk all day.

School gets serious

As September came, I entered the top class 7 taught by Mr Brooks. He was very strict and reminded me of "teacher" from the Beano's Bash Street Kids. His constant refrain was that the 11+ was fast approaching and we had to "buckle down". Dad added to the pressure by buying me a book of tests based on the exams which I obediently worked through.

Against one of the walls in the hall was the house leader board, indicating which house had the most points. There were three houses; Scott (red), Hillary (green) and my house Livingstone (yellow). In my final year I was honoured to be House Captain although I feel a little guilty having voted for myself in the secret ballot during the captain's election.

The school had a very interesting mix of pupils from different backgrounds, both in terms of ethnicity and relative wealth. I think it was about year 6 when Ernest Roper and his brother Lloyd arrived from Trinidad. They were the only two black boys in school at that time. Ernest was in my year and Lloyd the year below. It must have been a shock to come from the warmth of the Caribbean to our British weather and of course a totally different culture. I was friends with Ernest who was a very strong lad but had trouble with his flat feet which you could see by the difficulty he had both running and walking. It led to him taking many trips to Harvey Road school clinic. My weakness was my teeth as I spent so much time at the clinic, I knew the drill only too well.

Party time at Ernie's

Along with a small number of classmates I was invited to a birthday party at his house on Church Road just beyond the record shop and the model shop where we would buy our balsa wood.

The terraced house had a distinctive aroma that I put down to Caribbean cooking. Ernie's parents made us all very welcome and I was fascinated by the mechanical basketball game he had received as one of his presents.

I remember dancing with Susan Ball to "put your head on my shoulder" by Paul Anka, and she did. I am delighted to report that Sue and my classmate Peter Barker are now happily married and still living in Brum.

Boots on

Due to a shortage of boys my place in the school football team was guaranteed. We tried hard and actually won at least one game when I scored the winning goal against Cottesbrook Junior school. Dad came to watch most games and was very encouraging. One Saturday morning our goalkeeper was injured and I volunteered to go between the sticks. We were hammered and I had to retrieve the ball from the back of the net on several occasions. I was down beat but soon recovered as I received many consolatory words from teammates and supporters.

The Muscle man

The nation was captivated by Tony Holland on the popular ITV television talent show Opportunity Knocks hosted by Hughie Green. Tony, aged 25, performed his muscle moving act stripped to his bathing trunks and accompanied by "Wheels Cha Cha Cha". He won for six weeks on the trot and soon appeared at the Palladium. I used to perform my own version for to amuse friends and relatives.

Other events in 1964

January 1- Top of the Pops launched on BBC

January 21- Average weekly wage reaches £16

January 22- The film Zulu released

March 28- Pirate radio station Radio Caroline begins broadcasting from a ship off Felixstowe

March 30- Mods and Rockers clash on Clacton beach

April 1- Beatles Can't Buy me Love reaches Number 1 in UK charts

April 21- BBC 2 begins broadcasting its first programme; Play School

May 11- Terence Conran opens first Habitat store in London

May 29- the Bull Ring shopping centre opens as the first undercover shopping centre in the UK

July 1- First Brook Street Advisory Centre opened

July 6- Beatles first film A Hard Day's Night released

July 28- Winston Churchill retires as an MP aged 89

August 4- First portable televisions go on sale

August 13- Last UK hanging (Peter Allen)

August 22- Match of the Day launched on BBC2

September 4- Forth Road bridge opens

October 15- Labour win General Election and Harold Wilson becomes PM

November 2- The soap Crossroads begins

December 21- MPs vote to abolish the death penalty

90% of UK homes now own a TV (25% in 1953)

Best-selling single in 1964 Beatles Can't Buy Me Love selling 1.53 million copies

Chapter 9 1965: Big School beckons

Testing time

I was dreading the 11+ for two main reasons. The first was that Steve had sailed through it and was doing really well at Central Grammar School for Boys in Tile Cross. The second was the thought of having to go to Cockshut Hill Secondary Modern School if I failed. It had a rough reputation at the time although it probably wasn't anywhere near as bad as I imagined it to be.

The 11+ exam consisted of two papers testing verbal and non-verbal reasoning. They were both set for early February. I sat the first one and didn't think I had done too badly. The second paper followed a week later but unfortunately Nannah Piggott passed away the night before and the mood in our house was rather sombre. Mom decided that I should not sit the exam until something like normality had returned. I wasn't sure whether this was a good idea as I was keen to get the exams out of the way. Unfortunately, I had little choice in the matter. I spent the day helping Mom and Aunty Joyce tidy the bungalow as they searched for the necessary paperwork. I sat the second paper about a week later with a few others who had been ill during the previous week and had also missed the exam.

About 20% of those taking the exam in Birmingham were given a place at a grammar school. The key factor was the number of places available in the schools. In some areas of the country the pass rate was considerably lower than 20% as there were just not enough grammar school places.

When my success was confirmed my overwhelming feeling was one of relief. My Dad put Central as first choice as Steve was already there. When Steve passed in 1961 Central was chosen as it was recommended by Dad's best friend Peter Muddiman (AKA Uncle Peter). Both he and his twin brother Denis attended the school when it was located in the centre of town close to New Street station.

There was a bonus as when Steve passed Dad bought him a brand new bike which he rode the three miles to school each day as long as the weather was suitable. I politely declined the offer of a bike and negotiated a camera (Kodak instamatic 100) and a transistor radio to listen to the pirate radio stations particularly radio Caroline which was launched the previous year.

Confirmation of my acceptance at Central Grammar came through and all was right with the world, for now.

Taxing Spring

When Mom and Aunty Joyce sorted my Nan's affairs it was soon clear that our purchase of a fridge and washing machine may have been a little hasty. Although my Nan's savings were quite modest she had not declared any of it for quite some time. This meant the estate not only owed income tax but there was some over payment of state benefits to be reclaimed. After the numbers were calculated Mom was grateful to be able to keep her new machines and relieved that that slate was clean.

Out and about

In the summer of 1965, our class visited Blenheim Palace where Winston Churchill was born and Woodstock where he had been buried a few months earlier, following his death at the grand old age of 90 years. We also had a boat trip on the River Thames. It was a memorable day far more so than last year's trip to Coventry. I took lots of photographs on my new Kodak Instamatic 100. The photos were developed at Dad's office and the enlarged photos were pinned up on the wall in Mr Brooks' classroom. Sadly they were destroyed when two of my classmates broke into the school one night and ransacked several rooms. It was very near the end of term and the boys were caught straight away and did not return for the few remaining days.

Old Ma Vickers

At the end of the school day we would often call in at the nearest sweet shop next to the fishing tackle store. The Vickers shop sold a limited number of groceries but had plenty of sweets and ices. Old Ma Vickers, as we affectionately called her, also sold Lucky Bags. They were far from lucky as the contents were not worth the price, which I think was 3d. The toffee was rock hard, and the gifts were very poor quality. Sweets included liquorice reels, sweet cigarettes and coconut "tobacco". The ice-lollies were 1d for just flavoured ice or 2d for short stubby lollies containing a small amount of ice cream. Collectable cards were also for sale and very popular. There was a stampede when Topps American Civil War cards came on sale. In addition to the cards there was a fake dollar note. One denomination was particularly rare and was never seen by any of us.

They were happy days at Hobmoor and proved my Mom and Dad's choice to be a good one. A few years ago, the old school building was closed and the school was moved about half a mile down Hobmoor Road to a new site on the corner of Wash Lane. I hope the children there now have as good a time as we did.

Supermarket sweeps in

Our first supermarket had arrived in the form of Fine Fare. It was located at 129 Church Road just four doors down from Woolworths and next door to Geo Mason's. It had trolleys as well as baskets and seemed very modern. Mom stayed loyal to the Co-op and her divi but it proved popular. It had very competitive prices, own label products (Yellow packs), and a wide selection of products. Unique in the area was the added extra of PINK TRADING STAMPS.

Fine Fare had begun issuing their Pink stamps before Tesco entered the battle with GREEN SHIELD stamps. Both offers rewarded customers by issuing stamps based on the amount spent in their stores. These could be collected then redeemed for goods displayed in catalogues. Green Shield became the most popular and shops were opened where the stamps could be topped up with cash. These shops eventually turned into present day Argos stores. The Co-op also turned to stamps somewhat late in the day. The market changed when Tesco pulled out in favour of lower prices in 1977 reportedly saving £20 million.

Shopping at the Yew Tree

With the addition of Fine Fare, the Yew Tree was able to fulfil most shopping requirements even for an eleven year old. Woolworths provided Airfix kits and records. Sweets came from the Dorothy Box, my favourites being Lovells chocolate nougat. Haircuts were suffered at Norman Knight's on Stoney Lane next to Walls wallpaper shop. Chips came from Yew Tree fish bar which eventually doubled in size after purchasing the adjacent Pork shop. School uniform came from Jacksons outfitters next door to the Birmingham Municipal Bank where my tiny savings were nurtured. Tuff shoes from Marlone's (I never did get those shoes with the compass in the heel) and glasses from Farmers opticians next door. Last but not least was Proffitt and Westwood, the seed shop where I bought ammunition for my pellet gun.

Three legs of Man

Going to the Isle of Man was our first holiday with Aunty Joyce and Uncle Cyril and it was also our first two-week break. This major change may have been connected to the death of my Nan and the receipt of a few extra pounds. We still sent one case on in advance and went by train to catch the ferry from Liverpool for a 3 and a 1/2 hour journey across the Irish Sea. Aunty Joyce and Uncle Cyril were regular visitors to the island as Uncle Cyril had, at one time, a relative in Castletown.

On arrival we picked up the white Austin 1800 we had arranged to hire. It was a bit of a squeeze for the six of us, but Dad had not yet taken his driving test restricting us to just one car. We drove to Castletown and booked in at the Union Hotel. It was a pub that took in a small number of guests, and we were made very welcome. My Dad hardly ever visited a pub let alone stayed in one.

Knowing the island so well my Aunt and Uncle were able to show us all the best parts of the island. It had just about everything from lovely beaches, picturesque glens and impressive structures such as Castle Rushen in Castletown, where I was happy to pose in the stocks. Two railways, one steam and the other electric, helped movement around the island and the huge wheel at Laxey was an impressive sight.

I don't think my Dad had flown since his days in the RAF during the war. Right in the middle of our holiday he had to fly back to Birmingham for an interview for an internal promotion. I was impressed that the Co-op were arranging the flights. The job was to manage the transport function which looked after all the bread vans, milk floats and funeral cars. Unfortunately, Dad was unsuccessful, but he didn't show any signs of what must have been a huge disappointment.

One of my memories unrelated to the island itself was continually hearing the Byrds' number one single "Mr Tambourine Man". It seemed to be on my new transistor radio all the time, but I loved the Bob Dylan song. A great island and a great holiday, I didn't realise then how often I would return to those shores in future years.

On the road

Cars were starting to become more common with around 30% of households owning one and we were now no exception. Steve and I were so excited about the new acquisition. Well when I say new it was a second-hand Morris 1000. To us it was a Rolls Royce.

It is funny how we can often remember certain registration plates, this one was 9121 WD. It was black with two very fine red lines running from front to back just below the windows. It had four doors and red seats. Dad bought it from the CO-OP transport department. I am not sure if he got any divi on it!

Big school

The long summer break ended, and it was time to head to big school. My friends around the square told me to expect a tough first day at Central. There were stories of being taken to see the "blue goldfish". This was where you were forced to look down the toilet pan for the non-existent exotic fish before your head was flushed. Steve was a fifth former so I thought I would be well protected. I soon discovered that I would be coping alone.

There were two routes to Central from our house. I could catch the number 17 at the Yew Tree and get off at the terminus and walk for about 15 minutes down the Medway. Alternatively, I could take the number 11 to the Bull's Head at Stechford and then catch the number 14 which I would leave at the bottom of the Meadway.

On my first day I set off, closely following Steve. He turned left at the bottom of Rockingham Road which meant we were catching the number 11. All was fine until he met up with some friends as we boarded the number 14 outside the Bull's Head pub. After about 15 minutes they all stood up and got off. This didn't feel right, and it wasn't. They had exited two stops early at Glebe Farm as that was where the bus was terminating as a "special". I followed them down the Kitts Green Road and then they turned off to the left and came on to Gressel Lane passing Sir Wilfred Martineau school and reaching the entrance to Central Grammar. I was where I needed to be but had never come that way before. Steve never said a word and strode off. It was clear to me that Steve did not want to be seen nursing his little brother. I had no problem with that but thought he should at least make sure I knew where I was going.

I was in 1P with form teacher Mr Brian Hutton who had the strange nick name of "Crut". No one could explain the origins of this most unusual nickname. He was an excellent teacher with his main subject being geography. Fortunately, I didn't see any goldfish of any colour that day. The only strange thing I saw were about three of the 90 first year pupils wearing short trousers which the other 87 of us had left at primary school. One of the three was John Roden who became a good friend and remains so to this day. He still wears shorts but only when the weather encourages him to do so.

At the end of the school day I was delighted to avoid a return trip along the same unfamiliar route as my Dad was waiting to take us home in the new "Roller ". Dad had only just passed his driving test having let his licence lapse from before the war. We travelled at a safe speed and of course, there were no seat belts to fasten.

The run up to the end of the year exposed me to my first taste of rugby and cross country running, neither of which I fell in love with. We had two England international rugby players Sam Doble and Colin McFadyean teaching us. I had Doble for PE and games and McFadyean for history. I would eventually adjust to rugby but not cross country.

Mr Jones (aka Jonah) took us for music and at our first lesson he made us individually sing the notes he played on the piano following as he moved up the scale. When it came to my turn I managed to reach the highest note. This led me to be chosen to sing a solo of "See amid the winter snow" at the December Christmas Festival. I was shaking like a leaf but managed to perform to a satisfactory standard in front of a packed hall including friends and family. It must have been Ok as I was chosen again the next Christmas.

Other events in 1965

January 24- Sir Winston Churchill dies aged 90

March 11- Goldie the golden eagle recaptured after 13 days of freedom from London Zoo

April 6- TSR2 the nuclear bomber project cancelled

June 18- Alcohol limit in blood for driving to be introduced

July 27- Ted Heath becomes leader of Conservative party

July 29- Second Beatles film Help debuts

August 1- Cigarette advertising banned on television

August 21- First football substitute, Keith Peacock appears

September 21- Natural gas discovered in the North Sea

September 30- Gerry Anderson's Thunderbirds are go on ITV

October 1- Corgi introduced toy car model of James Bond's Aston Martin DB5

October 18- Magic Roundabout goes full circle for the first time at 17.50 on BBC1

October 21- Ian Brady and Myra Hindley charged with Moors murders

November 6- Race Relations Act introduced

November 29- Mary Whitehouse founds the National Viewers and Listeners Association just two weeks after the word F**K is used on TV for the first time

December 12- The Beatles last live gig in UK in Cardiff

December 22- 70 mph maximum speed limit introduced

Also

CSE exams introduced with the top grade being seen as a bottom grade O level pass

Mary Quant introduces the Mini Skirt in her Chelsea shop

The Rotunda building completed in Birmingham

Asda opens its first supermarket in Castleford Yorkshire

Pizza Express opens its first restaurant in London

Best-selling single in 1965 Ken Dodd's Tears, remaining at number 1 for 5 weeks and is the 3rd highest selling single in the 1960's. We even bought Mom a copy for her birthday.

Chapter 10 1966 - Going off track

Panto Treat

Before going back to school after the Christmas holidays Dad treated us to a family outing to see Ken Dodd and his Diddymen perform in the Humpty Dumpty panto at the Birmingham Hippodrome. Doddy did not disappoint. I was tickled and Mom loved his singing. He gave full value then and continued to keep audiences back way into the night over the next 50 years.

Singing in the Bull Ring

The redeveloped Bull Ring shopping centre had been open for a couple of years and in addition to a large number of shops and outdoor market it boasted a busy indoor market. One Saturday morning I met up with some new friends I had made at Central Grammar including Vince Barrow, Keith Florey plus a couple of others whose names have faded with time.

In the market hall we discovered a recording booth which enabled the making of 7-inch vinyl records. We excitedly pooled our pocket money to meet the necessary amount. I vaguely remember some discussion about what exactly we were going to record but as we crammed into the booth chaos ensued and somehow we broke into singing "Crut is a nut, Crut is a nut, ee aye addio Crut is a nut".

I have no idea where the inspiration to sing about my form teacher came from in such a ridiculous fashion, but the deed was done. The recording was automatically played back and seemed to include more random chatter and laughter than singing, nevertheless we were delighted with our recording debut. I have no idea who claimed the masterpiece, but, as far as I am aware, it has never resurfaced.

Cricket Captain

When the cricket season came around, I immediately put my name down for practice. At Hobmoor primary school I had been Captain and opened both the batting and the bowling. My prowess at such a tender age was due mainly to Dad's coaching… and the lack of boys in our class. At my new school there were 90 boys in my year providing plenty of competition. Despite problems with my vision I could still bat well but my ability to bowl seemed to have disappeared completely. My form teacher Mr Hutton (aka "Crut") took us for cricket and decided that I should share the captaincy with the very talented Johnny Tipper.

In the first of three matches against our local grammar schools I was selected to open the batting with the hard hitting left hander Keith Florey. Keith and I worked well together with his free scoring and my dogged defence at the other end. In our first match we put on 71 for the first wicket which was a record at the time. Overall, we won two and drew one of the matches. I loved being Captain and being able to try different tactics. I resolved to try and hold the position the following year.

"Don't forget, book early"

This phrase, delivered by owner Fred Pontin, ended each of the TV advertisements promoting Pontin's holiday camps. We had tried Butlin's and Warner's and it was time to follow Fred's plea. Pontin's marketed itself somewhere between Butlin's and Warner's which appealed to us. It was always going to be more fun for youngsters than the old YMCA.

Bracklesham Bay is in West Sussex on the South coast. As we now had our own car it was deemed reachable. We started out very early at about 6am as we had an exciting reason for getting there in good time.

They think it's all over

We arrived at Bracklesham Bay on Saturday 30th July 1966 as England were just about to kick off against West Germany in the World Cup final at Wembley. To our relief there was a large TV lounge on site. It was packed with people many of them from London supporting the three West Ham players; Hurst, Peters and Captain Bobby Moore. Steve and I sat on the floor right in front of the television that was larger than the one we would have been glued to at home. It was perched at a height of about five feet to enable the whole room to see the screen. The atmosphere was electric and the excitement peaked and troughed as the advantage shifted from one side to the other. It all came good at the end as Hurst thumped the ball home, making history. I can't really remember what happened next but know that celebrations around the camp continued well into the night.

In honour of the World Cup victory a football match was arranged by the Pontin's staff. I was disappointed to be told that it was for adults only. My Dad was 45 and not what you would consider fit. Mom was slightly alarmed when, under some pressure, Dad agreed to go in goal for one of the teams.

We watched anxiously as we knew he probably was the oldest person on the pitch and should not be playing. He did make a couple of decent saves which helped his side win 5-4. We had some fun when I pointed out to Mom that one of the defenders was a "sweeper" (the then fashionable description for a defender that played behind the other defenders to clear up any loose balls). "Does he work here as a cleaner" Mom enquired. It took us quite some time to explain the defensive position's common name.

It took Dad a couple of days to recover but the role was never to be repeated much to our collective relief. As we returned home we decided that Pontins was Ok but it was no Butlins.

Up the Swan quietly

My friend John Lavender was a prolific reader and devoured books. He was frequently found reading when I called for him. John enjoyed Dennis Wheatley books, particularly those concerning the occult. My interest was more focused on sport, particularly anything detailing cricket techniques. John and I often spent Saturday mornings walking the twenty-minutes up to the library close to The Swan pub. John always took out the maximum of four books which he would devour before the week was out while I returned home with a couple of sports books.

Bangers and mash

As bonfire night approached, I spent more time "up the field" i.e. the cricket field behind Heathmere Avenue. It was owned by Yardley Village Trust and rented out to the Marlborough Cricket Club who only used it at weekends during the summer months. It was a great place and became our unofficial playground whenever it was free.

One of the lads from the square would often call for Andrew Bullock on our way 'up the field' as his house in Heathmere Avenue backed on to the ground and had access through a gate at the end of his garden. One of the other sides of the field backed on to Clements Road, with the other two sides backing on to allotments and the Ashmore's derelict poultry farm. We generally stayed clear of the allotments apart from the pond in the corner where we liked to hunt for newts and frogs. The run-down poultry farm provided lots of cover for us to make dens and play hide and seek. The old wooden cricket pavilion was also a no-go zone. It always looked as if it was about to collapse so only the bravest of us (usually Alan Horton) would crawl under it in search of stray cricket balls with occasional success.

Under the influence of the older kids, mainly Alan Horton and Keith Jinks, we began to experiment with fireworks bought locally. Keith and Alan built a small cannon which worked quite effectively. We also began to somewhat recklessly light and throw bangers around, mostly missing each other! We also enjoyed firing rockets from the flat roof of the small toilet block located to the side of the pavilion. Firing the "mini rockets" was more like launching missiles and great fun unless one was coming your way.

One evening, when we had been mucking about for some hours, I accidently held on too long to a banger and it exploded right in front of me. Fortunately, I was wearing gloves and holding it at the very end of my outstretched arm. Even so some of the residue powder landed in my eyes causing them to smart and become irritated. I was forced to scurry home and through lack of an imaginative explanation for my injury I had to confess all. Not surprisingly my Dad was very cross and so was my Mom. Dad made an instant decision to take me to the eye hospital where I had previously been treated for my squint. I was lucky, as the nurse constantly reminded me. After clearing the specs of power from my eyes I was discharged with a tube of cream to apply for the next few days. I learned my lesson the hard way and was relieved to get away with just sore eyes and a good telling off.

On the drive

As bonfire night arrived we shared an enjoyable bonfire party with the Beresford's next door. We held a small bonfire in the shared drive. The two Dads Stan and Eric were in charge of lighting the fireworks with Moms Olive and Marjorie providing delicious food and hot drinks.

We always bought loose fireworks as they were better value than boxes and enabled more precise selection. Mom would take us to town where we would visit, yes, you've guessed it, the main Co-op high street store.

In the weeks leading up to bonfire night different fireworks would be displayed on sliding shelves in glass units providing us with a clear view of the many varieties. One of our favourites was called "Calling all Cars" which, when lit would let out a piercing noise mimicking a police siren. Catherine Wheels were also popular with us although they often needed a helping nudge from one of our Dads.

We held these shared celebrations for a number of years becoming an established tradition. They were a very different experience compared to messing around with fireworks with friends. I had learnt my lesson the hard way and was far more careful in the following years.

Collecting

I have always been a bit of a collector and started to turn my attention to postage stamps. Mr Beresford from next door encouraged me by giving me a generous bundle to start me off. Many of the stamps I received where from Africa as Eric regularly corresponded with missionaries out there. I was grateful for his help but in truth took more of an interest in collecting British stamps. I had three main sources: some used stamps came from Dad's office; some from "approvals" (bought through the post); and some from the Imperial shop on Church Road close to Wimbush's and the Belverdere greengrocers.

The Imperial was a sweet shop, a bit like the Dorothy Box on the other side of the road. In the Imperial's window it had two interesting displays. There was an extensive display of Matchbox cars and a colourful array of stamps neatly displayed in shiny transparent packets. I considered the cars far too small to be of interest as I preferred the larger Dinky and Corgi brands. However, the stamps did grab my attention and I became a regular buyer.

I became aware of 'approvals' in Steve's Victor comic. It was a simple process where I received a batch of stamps each month and could select to buy or return. Steve became interested too and we started to buy first day covers of each new issue of British stamps. My stamp collecting carried on into my twenties and I still have them all neatly packed away.

Becoming a hooker

During the school winter term, I was selected for the school rugby team. As I was relatively small in comparison to the rest of the squad I was placed in the middle of the front row as hooker. I had two tall and strong props, Murray and Williams who provided excellent support. We were a successful team and often received strong praise in the school magazine "The Hammer". I must admit that sometimes I did find myself ending up in the opposition's half of the scrum but in general we won more scrums than we lost.

I also found myself performing a solo again at the Christmas concert this time singing the Coventry Carol accompanied by a guitarist called King. I'm not sure how good I was but I can remember enjoying performing. I was certainly less nervous second time around. My confident performance in school encouraged me to carol sing locally to raise a few shillings (stamp buying funds) although my mom thought of such tin rattling as begging, as she did with "penny for the guy" which I was not allowed to take part in.

Staying on track

For as long as I can remember I had wanted a Scalextric car racing set for Christmas but was told each year that they were too expensive. Steve and I tried a new tactic and asked if we could share our main present. Much to our delight Dad agreed and came up with the much wanted Scalextric set. We were so excited as we scrambled to assemble the circuit on Christmas Day.

Once it was completed we expectantly pressed the hand controls. Nothing happened. We checked all the joints and wires again but could not find a fault in our construction. We just couldn't get it going. I was so disappointed that I shouted out something I regret to this day; "this is the worst Christmas I have ever had". How could I say that after all my Dad had done to grant my wish? Thankfully my parents seemed to understand my frustration and set about trying to solve the problem.

Help was soon at hand in the shape of Dad's best friend Peter Muddiman who we affectionately called Uncle Peter. He always came around for an hour or so on Christmas Day on his way to pick up his sister Nora. He was often accompanied by one of his three children, Linda, Julia or Andrew. As Peter worked in the same office as Dad he knew about the Scalextric and had brought us two Scalextric accessories, a control tower and a grandstand. Better still he managed to fix the problem and get it working and that was us hooked for the rest of the holiday.

The circuit was packed away at the end of the festive period. Later I managed to set a smaller circuit up in my bedroom as Steve had moved into the box room. Given the size of the circuit part of the track ran under my bed. It was a problem finding the space to experience the full benefit and it came out of its box less and less and was sold a couple years later.

On the telly

As usual we all looked forward to TV during the festive season and it was the only time we bought the Radio Times. It added to the excitement by including two weeks' schedule including all the New Year programmes. Christmas TV featured one of my Dad's favourites "The Black and White Minstrels" featuring soloists Dai Francis, John Boulter and Tony Mercer. There were also comedy routines featuring Leslie Crowther, George Chisholm and Stan Stennett.

The show was extremely popular, often been viewed by over 20 million people. Another of Mom and Dad's favourites was Dr Finlay's Casebook which was strangely broadcast at 10.30pm. I was keen to watch the final episode of the first series of Thunderbirds at 5pm narrowly avoiding a clash with tea.

Another regular Christmas TV event was a Brian Rix farce. The 1966 farce from the Whitehall Theatre was "One for the Pot" which had run for over 1000 productions since 1964.

I can remember this being another happy Christmas despite my unfortunate outburst.

Other Events in 1966

January 30- Action Man toy figures introduced

March 4- John Lennon says "Beatles more popular than Jesus now"

March 27- Pickles the dog finds the stolen World Cup trophy (Jules Rimet)

March 30- Labour win General Election

April 6- First cross channel hovercraft service begins

June 6- Sitcom "Till death us do part "begins

June 29- Barclays Bank introduces the first British credit card, "Barclaycard"

August 29- Beatles play their very last concert in Candlestick Park San Francisco

October 21- Aberfan disaster kills 144

Best-selling single in 1966 Tom Jones' "The Green Green grass of Home" spent seven weeks at Number 1 and sold over one million copies

Chapter 11 1967: Venturing abroad

Beanz Meanz Heinz

TV advertising was in full swing with music playing an increasing important role in hooking customers to products. Many of the old adverts come back so easily due to the musical link. How many of the following spark a tune in your head?

"Trebor Mints are a minty bit stronger"

"Hands that do dishes can feel soft as your face with mild green Fairy Liquid"

"P..P..Pick up a Penguin, P..P..Pick up a Penguin, when you feel a little bit peckish P..P..Pick up a Penguin"

"If you like a lot of chocolate on your biscuit join our Club"

"Opal fruits, made to make your mouth water"

"Ticker, ticker Timex TRA LA LA!"

"This is luxury you can afford from Cyril Lord"

"One thousand and one cleans a big big carpet for less than half a crown"

"Everyone's a Fruit and Nut case"

And of course, the classic Cadbury Flake advert; "Only the crumbliest tastiest chocolate tastes like chocolate never tasted before".

There were of course many, many more but how deep seated they are in our minds.

Tuned in

I loved listening to comedy shows on the radio particularly on Sunday afternoons at 2pm after Family Favourites ended. I would lie on the settee in the lounge which came into use on Sundays and tune in. The "Navy Lark" had been running for years but was as popular as ever. It starred Leslie Phillips and John Pertwee aboard HMS Troutbridge. Leslie Phillips always found a way to voice his catch phrase "a touch of the old left hand down a bit".

The "Clitheroe Kid" starring Jimmy Clitheroe was also a regular Sunday afternoon programme featuring Jimmy as a schoolboy tormenting daft Alfie. "Round the Horne" starring Kenneth Horne provided more sophisticated humour that built on the previous hit "Beyond our Ken". The troubled yet talented Kenneth Williams added much to the show with Rambling Sid Rumpo and his camp partnership with Hugh Paddick in "Julian and Sandy".

I.S.I.R.T.A

I enjoyed all those old shows but my favourite was "I'm Sorry I'll Read That Again". It was a breeding ground for new talent such as Tim Brooke-Taylor, John Cleese, Graeme Garden, David Hatch, Jo Kendall and Bill Oddie.

 Before the ability to record programmes, Steve and I used to sit listening to ISIRTA with pens poised ready to capture any gems so we could repeat them at school. For example; during the professor's flying trousers sketch; "we are going to create a library at the bottom of his trousers", "that'll be a turn up for the books"! I know, but we thought it was so original and clever.

It's a record

The Sound of Music film starring Julie Andrews and Christopher Plummer was released in 1965. Critical response was mixed but the public loved it. It was so popular in Birmingham that it ran for 168 weeks at the Gaumont cinema on Colmore Circus. Dad bought the soundtrack album but you had to book so far in advance to see the film that Mom and Dad had to wait nearly two years before they were able to see it, accompanied by Aunty Joyce and Uncle Cyril.

Boys will be boys

My local friends now included Gary Durant (Gaz), Terry Twinberrow (Tez) and Paul Wells (Shrimp, he was the youngest and smallest at the time). They all lived on Stoney Lane and backed on to my road, Charminster Avenue. John Lavender's next-door neighbour Brian Harris also joined us. We spent a lot of time "up the field" which we could enter from Stoney Lane by a track next to the row of lock up garages that were beginning to deteriorate. We played football, cricket, built dens and lay on the grass in the sun.

During the Easter holidays we decided to venture into town to visit "The Boys and Girls Exhibition" at Bingley Hall on Broad Street. The Hall was built in 1850 and was used for circuses, exhibitions and later rock concerts.

The "Boys and Girls exhibition" had lots of interesting features. The RAF ran a parachute jump that replicated landing from a jump by rapidly lowering you from a towering platform to the ground. It was well controlled, but it still made your heart pound as you stood at the top of the scaffolding waiting to jump.

There was a mock-up of the popular "Juke Box Jury" which we took part in and were given a single disc that we had never heard of as a prize. The DJ was Dave Cash who was working on radio Luxembourg but would later join Radio 1.

What a picture

There were lots of stalls at the exhibition selling magic tricks, football programmes and of course food and drinks. There was a very interesting art stall that had a constant crowd of onlookers. As we gently joined the crowd the first thing I noticed was a strong smell of paint. Peering over the adjacent bodies I could see a metal container about 18 inches square. It was open at the top but at the bottom there was a circular disc about 9 inches in diameter. The stall holder attached a piece of card to the disc and closed a lid. A button was pressed, and the box vibrated as the disc and card rotated. The stall holder picked up a bottle of what turned out to be paint and squirted it through a gap in the lid. He repeated this with other colours and then switched the circulation off. After waiting a couple of minutes, he carefully recovered the card and held it up for us to see the result. There was a gasp and then applause. It was a striking piece of abstract art with strong vibrant colours leaping out across the card. I just had to have one. I did and treasured it for many years. Despite my reputation as a hoarder I have no idea where it went.

It was a good day out for the boys. Bingley Hall went on to hold many more exhibitions and rock concerts before it burnt down in 1984 and was later replaced by the International Convention Centre.

Janus makes a brief appearance

Gaz announced excitedly that his family (Mom, Dad, three older brothers and a younger sister) had acquired a dog. Not just any old dog but a Great Dane. He was called Janus after the Roman god of beginnings and endings.

We couldn't wait to meet up with him and take him for a walk. When we called round we were shocked as Gary tried to open the back door. He managed to create a small gap but Janus was towering above him with his front legs on each of Gaz's shoulders.

He was huge. Somehow we got his lead on and stumbled out into the drive. The idea was to take him for a walk; however Janus was in charge and was pulling Gaz along. We met Tez alongside his push bike on Stoney lane. After a few strides Tez leapt onto his bike and began to peddle. Janus went into overdrive at the sight of the wheels going around and Gaz was hanging on for dear life. John Lavender and I quickly grabbed hold of the lead and brought the huge animal under some sort of control.

We returned to Gaz's house and shut Janus inside. We relaxed thinking the situation was back under control and wandered up to the Dorothy box for ice creams. On our return Gaz came running out to announce that whilst we away Janus had eaten the settee. I think destroyed was a more apt description. Janus the Roman god of beginnings and endings was now about to end his short stay.

Lost in France

Back at the start of my second year at Central GS we had been invited to go on a week long trip to Paris. The cost was £20 and we were to pay £1 each week through into 1967. Mom and Dad were happy to support me as they thought it would be beneficial to both my French and wider education. The time soon came around for about 30 or 40 of us split equally from years 2 and 3 to venture abroad.

Outside the school we queued up to place our cases in the hold of the coach. One boy from my year didn't have a case to load but was clutching a brown paper carrier bag. Tucked inside the bag was a ragged looking school white shirt and a pair of pants and socks. My family were not well off but I felt so sorry for the lad as I compared his belongings with my packed case.

Only here for the beer

After a calm ferry crossing and uneventful coach journey we arrived at our accommodation in Paris.

It was a boarding school in the centre of the city. The pupils had returned home during the holidays making room for the adventurous Brummies. The dormitories were fairly basic but clean with reasonably comfortable beds. The food was also adequate with the added bonus of a small quantity of beer served with our evening meal. One evening a lad managed to consume more than his fair share leading to his uncontrollable giggling before he was marched off to bed by one of our teachers.

Discovering a weakness

We visited all the main sites. The Eiffel Tower was interesting but I soon discovered a problem with heights. The lift to the very top was a sort of cage with a clear view which I found distinctly uncomfortable. But this was nothing compared to my response to exiting on to the platform at the very top. I clung on to the outside of the lift area unable to move. I could not take in the view as I continued to press my back against the lift area. It seemed like forever before we re-entered the lift for the welcome descent.

In the Louvre we gathered around the Mona Lisa staring at the eyes that were meant to follow you. Not sure that they did or was it due to my dodgy eyesight? Notre Dame cathedral was impressive as was the Sacre-Coeur Basilica.

On the last day we were given a choice of visits and I chose Orly airport about seven miles outside the capital. I can't remember the alternative; it must have been pretty uninteresting if I chose the airport. There was nothing much to see other than lots of airplanes.

Bit of a fag

I was not a smoker but had been persuaded to bring back some cigarettes. They were easy to obtain and I had bought a packet of Peter Stuyvesant which I was hoping to sell at a profit.

As we approached the ferry to return home panic set in as the teachers warned us that we would probably be searched when boarding. The scare tactics worked and hasty dumping took place. It was a bluff that annoyingly saw me lose the chance to make a few bob but I suppose I deserved it.

Every picture tells a story

Back home Mom and Dad were keen to hear all about the trip. I had enjoyed my first visit outside the UK and went into much detail. When asked about the differences to Brum I told them that I could not recall seeing any birds. The feathered variety that is. I felt more than a little daft when my photographs revealed flocks of birds around the Sacre Coeur! I decided not to mention that we hardly spoke a word of French during the whole trip other than asking the waiters for "plus de biere.

I don't think Dad was too pleased when my school report revealed my position in French at 22 out of a class 22 with the comment "cheerfully incompetent". I have to admit I was.

A full season

The cricket season soon came around and I was really pleased to be made skipper of the under 13s. We played eight matches and only lost one. If our bowling had been more accurate we could have had a clean sweep. I was delighted to be mentioned in the school Magazine "The Hammer" for my batting and fielding.

I loved fielding at silly point (i.e very close to the batsman, square of the crease) where I caught several catches thanks to my Dad's hours of practice with me in the garden. I also enjoyed moving the field around, experimenting and trying to unsettle the batsman. It was great fun and good early "management" experience.

A leap too far

During the main summer holidays we began a game of leaping along the low wall outside John Lavender's house. It was built of concrete blocks each about 9 inches square. There were two bottom rows and then a row which included an alternate gap of one block all the way along. The game was to jump across the gaps from one end to the other. John lived at 12 Rockingham Road but the wall extended right across number 14 where our friend Brian Harris lived. The leaping soon attracted a crowd of participants and each day the challenge to jump further and faster grew. At the end of the week I was off to Eastbourne YM for one week followed by a further week at Butlins, Bognor Regis.

Side-lined

We drove down to Eastbourne and were greeted by glorious sunshine. After checking in Steve and I made our way on to the crowded beach just across the road from the Victoria Court YM. As always, I had a football and we began to try to head the ball to each other. I remember climbing up to head the ball and felt an incredible pain in my stomach. I was doubled up in pain with tears rolling down my face. Steve shepherded me back across the road in search of Mom and Dad.

I was in such agony that a doctor was called for and luckily one came even though it was a Saturday afternoon. I had a lump in my stomach and the doctor declared that I had torn a stomach muscle which had been weakened by the wall leaping. Bed rest and very limited activity for a couple of weeks or more. The timing could not have been worse on day one of a 14-day holiday with so many activities to be enjoyed at Butlins. I had no choice other than to comply as the pain restricted movement to such an extent. Towards the end of the second week I was able to dip in the pool but could not swim. I made the most of sitting and watching the entertainment but resolved to be more careful in future.

In the scrum

On return to school I did play for the rugby team who had a good season but my enthusiasm was beginning to wane. Physically I was not getting much bigger and this was proving to be a disadvantage in rugby. My days on the freezing winter pitches were numbered as I looked forward to swapping rugby for basketball as a winter sport.

Other events in 1967

January 4- Donald Campbell killed on Lake Coniston in an attempt to break the land speed record

January 7- The Forsyte Saga begins on BBC 2

February 26- Lightning strikes Highgate Town football pitch resulting in one player losing his life and three injured

March 29/30- Stricken oil tanker "Torrey Canyon" bombed by RAF

March 31- Jimi Hendrix sets fire to his guitar on stage and suffers burns to his hands

April 8- "Puppet on a String" performed by Sandie Shaw becomes the first English language song to win the Eurovision Song Contest

May 28- Francis Chichester arrived in Plymouth after completing his single-handed sailing voyage around the world

June 1- Beatles release "Sgt Pepper" album

July 1- Colour television broadcasts begin

August 27- Beatles manager Brian Epstein dies

September 20- QE 2 launched at Clydebank

September 30th- Radio 1 launched and other BBC stations renamed

November 28- Outbreak of foot and mouth stops horse racing

December 11- Concord aircraft unveiled in Toulouse

December 22- BBC radio panel game 'Just A Minute" hosted by Nicolas Parsons begins

Ford announce the end of production of the Anglia (my Uncle Cyril's car at the time)

Best-selling single in 1967 Engelbert Humperdinck "Please release me" spent six weeks at Number 1 and sold over one million copies

Chapter 12 1968: Educated by Helga

A shoe in

Dad used to go to work in town most Saturday mornings and he asked me if I would like to work at the Co-Op High Street store. At 14 I could only work for 3 or 4 hours which fitted in with Dad's working pattern. I was very nervous as Dad introduced me to the manager of the shoe department of the High Street store who was clearly a friend of Dad's. The manager was in his forties, but the rest of the staff were only a few years older than me. I was constantly teased which I soon got used to and was good training for later life. They offered me sex education by secretly passing me the notes from inside a pack of Durex condoms. I carefully hid them to read at home. The tiny, neatly folded sheets took ages to read and when I got to the end I knew all the terms and conditions which applied to the product but my sex education had not moved on at all.

Back in the shoe department I was informed that certain shoes carried a bonus if I managed to sell them. Such shoes had a distinctive mark on the front of the box which had to be torn off and handed to the manager at the end of a successful sale. They were of course old stock that needed moving on. I did try to sell some but not surprisingly they were usually ones that no one wanted.

Stand and deliver

After a few weeks my venture into sales ended when I was released from the shoe department as my Dad didn't want to work every Saturday morning. It had been a learning experience however I was pleased to be released from that world only really missing the canteen.

The newspaper shop next to the chip shop on Stoney Lane was always looking for paperboys, but Mom and Dad weren't keen as they thought it would have an adverse impact on my schoolwork.

I wasn't too keen on getting up early in cold weather either. By this time my friend Tez and his sister Ann were helping out at the newsagents on Church Road near the Swan. They offered me two weeks work as a relief paperboy at the Easter break. Helping out during the holidays meant no impact on school. Even better, it was the afternoon delivery of the Birmingham Evening Mail so I avoided early rising.

The "round" was very close to the Swan pub, including Emily Road, and most of the houses took the paper. It was an exceptionally warm Easter and the terraced houses had a lobby which let them leave the front door open with another door about a yard further back. The front gardens were tiny and I found that I could roll the papers up and toss them into the lobby without damaging them. It was a breeze and I found myself whistling as I enjoyed the round.

During the summer holidays I performed a similar role for the Stoney Lane newsagents covering for the boys on family holidays. I even delivered our own papers for two weeks.

On trial in a frock

As a member of the school choir I was an automatic choice for the school's first attempt at opera albeit the light-hearted Gilbert and Sullivan "Trial by Jury". The downside was having to dress as a woman in the public gallery. My brother Steve, not noted for his vocal talent, was to my surprise found as a member the Jury.

It was a relatively short single act performance only lasting about an hour. It was great fun to be part of and rehearsals often broke down into fits of laughter. At one point the soloist sings "I have one word my lord and that is rapture". But during one rehearsal he sang "I have one word my lord and that is RUPTURE". Everyone laughed, even the teachers Sandiland and Hutton could not help but join in. On many future occasions there would be sniggering when the same phrase arose. However, it was all right on the night. Amazingly us "girls" escaped any micky taking for our attire.

An English summer

I was pleased to be made cricket captain again and was looking forward to a successful season. During the winter our teacher Brian Samways (main subject Physics) had squashed us in his van and taken us to the indoor cricket school at Edgbaston the home of Warwickshire CCC. It was a great experience which he shared out amongst the squad of players.

We were due to play eight matches against other schools but unfortunately the weather intervened. The rain came and we only managed to complete half of our planned matches. I can remember sitting next to Dad as we drove down the Meadway on our way to the school playing fields. We saw my friend John Roden, the team scorer, cycling through the pouring rain. We stopped and suggested that he tuned his bike round and head for home as there seemed little chance of the match being played. He didn't take much persuading.

We won two drew one and lost one. The team played well with a great team spirit. Graham Buckley was a fine all-rounder and scored a superb 54 and took 6 wickets for 14 as we thrashed Waverley by 69 runs. Vice-captain Keith Florey (aka Floss) scored an attacking 36 in a drawn match against King Edwards Aston where I chipped in with a relatively sedate 20. The match we lost was against King Edwards Nuneaton where Derek Savage scored 18 and took 5 wickets for 15 runs. A short but enjoyable season.

Silver celebrations

My parents were married in June 1943 just before my Dad was posted to Egypt for the last two years of the war. They honeymooned in Broadstairs on the Kent coast. This June was their silver anniversary and they decided to celebrate with a few days in London staying at the Strand Palace Hotel.

They had tickets to Wimbledon; court one on Friday and centre court on Saturday. They saw Roy Emerson and Pancho Gonzales on the Friday. Then Manuel Santana, Owen Davidson and Lew Hoad on the Saturday. They also had passes to a refreshment enclosure. I suspect Dad obtained these via the tennis section at the Co-op sports club where he had been secretary.

On Friday evening they had seats in row D at the Victoria Palace theatre to see Dad's favourite show, the Black and White Minstrels. This was of course before political correctness had surfaced. On Saturday evening they had reservations at the revolving restaurant on top of the GPO tower which had been opened two years earlier. Somewhat surprisingly it was run by Butlin's, not usually one of Dad's favourite organisations. They obviously had a great time as they kept all the tickets and brochures enabling me to accurately reproduce their itinerary.

Steve and I were packed off to Aunt Joyce and Uncle Cyril's house at Bacons End on the Chester Road. It was close enough to walk to school on the Friday. We were very well looked after at the Potters. Aunt Joyce produced her famous potato swirls which we simply loved. She would mash potatoes and then put them in an icing bag and squeeze the contents out in a circular movement building up to a point. The swirls were then baked in the oven to be removed with a slightly tinged edge. How boring ordinary potatoes would be after that.

Food for thought

When we returned home our food returned to its normal pattern;

Sunday; Roast dinner at lunchtime. Either well done beef and Yorkshire pudding cooked flat and square with gravy, not jam as sometimes appears further north. Other meats included roast chicken and pork. Veg was usually peas (in season I would enjoy removing them from their pods) always accompanied by carrots. No sign of broccoli but often green beans appeared in season.

Monday; Out came the mincer to attack the leftovers from the Sunday roast. A pie was topped with potato and often partnered by baked beans.

Tuesday; Liver and onions

Wednesday; Often time for a stew to appear.

Thursday; Time for chops, either lamb or more often pork as they were bigger for the three hungry chaps to consume.

Friday; Egg beans and chips but no fish, although fish fingers made an infrequent appearance. I always added cheese to the usual meal leading to my Mom's eyebrows reaching new heights.

Saturday; Could be anything depending on our activities. In the winter we often had baked potatoes cooked under the grate amongst the ash, until a gas fire was introduced.

Puddings;
Bananas in custard; These appeared in glass dishes placed in the fridge. If any of the banana slices appeared above the custard, they turned black but were still eaten without complaint.

Semolina and jam; I never liked this and made sure there was plenty of jam to disguise the taste.

Angels Delight; Full of sugar and carbs but went down a treat, especially butterscotch. Easily superior to its rival Instant Whip.

Blancmange; Similar to the Angels Delight but probably cheaper. Came in traditional flavours and best eaten after cooled in the fridge.

Birds lemon meringue pie; This usually only appeared on Sundays or special occasions. It was one my favourites, as was Birds trifle that definitely only made it to the table as a real treat.

When there were no puddings there would be cake. The regulars were Battenberg and chocolate rolls. I scoffed a lot of biscuits often swallowed with vast quantities of orange squash leading to more visits to the school dentist in Harvey Road. Incidentally I recently discovered by reading one of Professor Carl Chinn's excellent books (The Streets of Brum part 2) that Harvey Road was called Donkey Lane up until 1906. My favourite biscuits were Nice and Sports followed closely by the more expensive Penguin bars and Wagon wheels.

It isn't Butlins

I was told that I had been to the Skegness YMCA family holiday centre before. As I was only two years old at the time I had absolutely no recollection of the visit. I was surprised how good it was. Easily the best of the YM's we had been to. I couldn't understand why we had not been here for twelve years. It had a huge grass area for both cricket and football. A small sports hall for table tennis and children's activities. A ballroom where dancing and other entertainment took place. It was in a lovely setting with a wooded area and was only a ten minute walk from the beach, although it might be another ten minutes to reach the sea if the tide was out.

The only downside was that Steve was now learning to drive and there were some scary moments. On the plus side I was starting to take an interest in girls and her name was Ann.

She lived in the same road as the YM. It was all very innocent, and I can remember my Dad finding my besotted look highly amusing. We danced together in step doing the "March of the Mods", (forwards, backwards, one two three). I was so taken that I imagined seeing her after we got back home. I was really taken with "Skeggy" and vowed to return.

Laughing policeman

In September I entered the 4th form and soon realised that life was now very different. My brother had left at the end of last term after completing his A levels. I was surprised that although he was successful in passing History and English, he failed French. He had never had a failure before although he didn't seem too bothered as he had been offered a management trainee position with Lloyds Bank at their Priory Circus branch in the city centre and he had already started. This was a more serious time at school as I had embarked on my O level subjects but my attitude towards schoolwork was still far from focused. I seemed to think that I could wander along and all would come good in the end.

I strolled home from school without a care in the world and turned my key in the front door. As it opened I froze instantly as a complete mess greeted me. I shouted out to my Mom. As there was no reply I suddenly remembered that she had gone in to town to meet Aunt Joyce. I backtracked at speed and went next door to the Beresfords at number 11. Mrs B came around and soon doubled back to call the police.

They came quickly and after a look round declared the house safe. The burglars had broken through the back door where we had obligingly left a key on the inside of the lock. There was glass all over the floor from the broken window.
The rest of the house was a mess with every drawer tipped out. Mom appeared next and was naturally upset. Dad and Steve were not far behind.

The police dusted for prints but seemed to lose interest when we decided that nothing was missing. Not that there was much to take. The police took a small black box that they thought may have relevant prints. It was never seen again. Security was tightened by deciding it was not a good idea to leave the sun lounge unlocked and a key in the back door.

Playing out

When not up the field, the boys sometimes hung out at the shops. Hardings Bakery on Church Road near the Swan had been sold and was being redeveloped into the Tivoli Shopping Centre. A few of us decided to have a look at how the work was progressing. To our surprise it was close to being completed. Security was about as good as we had applied at home i.e. non-existent. We soon found our way into the empty shops through loose boarding and were fascinated by internal access down to a deserted central loading bay. We crept around the darkened areas like Zombies in the night. Our fun didn't last long as some of the units became inhabited by living shop keepers. We were soon back up the field with our music guru Brian Harris (lived at 14 Rockingham Road next door to John Lavender). Brian had acquired a mobile record player and was widening his musical interest from Jimi Hendrix, through the Moody Blues to a brief fling with reggae. Brian's interest in music was to our benefit as he introduced us to new bands. Live performances were not far away.

Sex education

No formal sex education was provided at our school. Playground chat could certainly not be relied on. Biology lessons skipped around the topic leaving us to study the well-thumbed pages covering human reproduction in "Introduction to Biology". Back home was no better and some of us decided to take matters into our own hands.

We went to the Futurist cinema in John Bright Street to see the German-made sex education film "Helga". It has since been described by some as a porn movie for teenagers. To me it was a factual documentary on reproduction, more like the textbook pages brought to life. When I got home my Dad asked me if I had any follow up questions for him. I wasn't embarrassed, I really didn't have any suitable questions at that time. If pushed I could have just asked as to where I could find a Helga!

A week later I was watching "The Graduate" at the Beaufort cinema with my school friend Mark Ford and couldn't decide which film was the more informative!

Other events in 1968

January 8- PM Harold Wilson launches "I'm backing Britain" campaign.

March 17- Demonstration in Grosvenor Square against Vietnam war

April 18- London Bridge sold to be rebuilt in Arizona

April 20- MP Enoch Powell makes "Rivers of Blood "speech

April 27- Abortion legalised

May 3- Britain's first heart transplant

May 29- Manchester United become the first British winners of the European Cup

June 8- Martin Luther King's killer James Earl Ray arrested at Heathrow airport

July 31- Dad's Army begins on BBC

August 11- Britain's last steam train service runs

August 31- First Isle of Wight pop festival

September16- First and second class post introduced

September 27- The musical "Hair" opens in London

October 2- Britain's first sextuplets born in Birmingham

November 21- Carpet firm Cyril Lord goes into receivership (luxury you can no longer afford)

Best-selling single in 1968 Beatles "Hey Jude" selling over five million copies worldwide

Chapter 13 1969   Growing up fast

Tragedy strikes

At first, we thought it was funny that Dad had been diagnosed with "Hong Kong Flu". That all changed a few days later. On Monday 3rd February I returned home from school in high spirits as I had just booked my coach to London to watch Villa play Spurs in the FA Cup at White Hart lane. I was surprised to find my Dad's parents and Aunt Joyce and Uncle Cyril sat in the front room. "Family gathering?" I enquired not thinking anything was wrong.

I was shepherded into the living room by my Aunt where Mum was sitting looking very sad. They gently explained that my Dad had suffered a fatal heart attack after parking his car in town. I immediately asked where my brother was as he would have been with him. Steve was kept at the hospital as he was suffering from severe shock having witnessed the terrifying event. I was numb and didn't know quite what to do. I was relieved when Steve came home but not surprisingly, he disappeared to his bedroom.

The cremation was booked for Friday 7th at Yardley Cemetery. In the chaos mum had forgotten that this was Steve's nineteenth birthday, but it was too late to change it. It snowed heavily on the day with the front lawn strewn with flowers on top of several inches of snow. The crematorium was packed but I couldn't really take it in. Afterwards at the house it was just family and close friends. The board of directors from the Co-op made a brief appearance and I remember one of them, Mrs Christmas, telling me I now had to look after my Mom, as if I wouldn't!

 Both Steve and I stayed at home that week trying to come to terms with events. Dad knew he had health problems not helped by his 40 a day habit but obviously did not realise that his mitral valve was badly damaged. Today it would have been found and treated, possibly with a valve replacement.

I spent time desperately trying to remember our last words and even what he looked like. It was a tough time with the mind playing all sorts of tricks, even denying he had actually died.

To add to our woes within weeks Mom had a hysterectomy. Even worse Aunt Joyce and Uncle Cyril were committed to moving to a brand-new bungalow on the Isle of Man following Uncle Cyril's retirement. My Dad's mum, Nannah Duffin, was devastated by the loss of her only son at 48 and never really recovered, passing away less than two years later.

Mom made an appointment to see Dad's GP Dr Barber who reassured her that it was not likely to be passed on to her sons and was mainly down to smoking. Steve and I never smoked. I experimented calling it a day after foolishly smoking a Wills Wiff up the field and throwing up.

Back to school

Returning to form 4P brought some normality back to my disturbed life. The school were sympathetic and helpful. My Dad had helped the school by supplying excess and old cricket equipment from the Co-op sports club and got to know one of the teachers, Taffy Thomas, who lived on Stoney Lane. Taffy wrote a lovely letter to my Mom which she very much appreciated.

I was summoned to see the school secretary and surprised that help was at hand. Due to our poor financial situation i.e no income other than the state widows' pension and a tiny Co-op pension, I was entitled to free school meals and a clothing allowance to help with school uniform, PE kit etc. The Co-op had paid out on my Dad's death in service which only just covered the mortgage but there was no other life insurance. Steve was able to help a little and I decided to look for a Saturday job.

All the way to Pool Way

Dad's best friend and work colleague Uncle Peter Muddiman arranged for me to work Saturdays at the Co-op supermarket in the Pool Way shopping centre. It was about a ten-minute bike ride. I had heard of a gang from the area that I thought was called the Paul Way mob I soon realised my error. The manager was Mr Fox who rarely left his den, perched at the end of the long row of checkouts.

One Saturday the assistant manager Mr Rooke (aka Rooky) instructed me to refill the margarine tubs. When it came to one brand the tubs came in packets of two and had to be separated for single sales. I noticed that the double packs had an offer for Zorbit towels. The packet covers to be thrown away contained a voucher which I removed before placing them in the huge bins. From that moment on I made that area of the shop my own and refilled as often as I could. I sent the towels to relatives as well as home. The postman was very busy and it was quite a while before I threw in the towel.

Having a small weekly income of £1-4/- made me feel I was contributing something to the household as I could buy some clothes and not need any pocket money. The only downside of my Saturday job was missing out on playing cricket for the school and I really missed it.

Pirates on parade

It was helpful to have something to concentrate on at this time and our second Gilbert and Sullivan light opera, The Pirates of Penzance went live at the end of March. It was great fun to be one of the pirates crossing the stage "with cat like tread". One of the other pirates was the now well-known actor Kevin McNally best known for playing Joshamee Gibbs in all of the Pirates of the Caribbean films. Once a pirate always a pirate!

I later met Kevin at the Olivier Awards where Sue and I were guests of the sponsors, American Express. At the end of the night Kevin and I drunkenly revived "with cat like tread" in front of his wife Phyllis Logan, known for her performances as Mrs Hughes in Downton Abbey and earlier as Lady Jane in Lovejoy. I am not sure Kevin remembered me but he put on a convincing performance.

Share and share alike

There were huge changes at the Villa. A new board had taken over with the ambitious Doug Ellis as chairman. "deadly Doug" as he became known had made his money in the travel business owning Sunflight which provided package holidays. One of his first changes gave me a decision to make.

The board decided to issue new shares in the club at £5 per share. My wealth had reached £15 by the time the prospectus dropped through the letterbox. Apart from the possibility of the share value increasing there were two other potential benefits. Shareholders would be given a discount on season tickets and preference for tickets to cup finals. I would have bought one share even without the added incentives. Although I declined to buy a season ticket, I did use the ticket preference for finals on at least three occasions. It is remarkable that this £5 investment turned out to give a whopping return of £500 when the club was sold to American billionaire Randy Lerner for £62.6million in 2006.

Out of this world

There was excitement as the American spacecraft Apollo 11 landed on the Moon towards the end of July. Mom woke us up just before dawn to watch Neil Armstrong take his "giant leap for mankind". It was very strange to be watching Armstrong and Buzz Aldrin making history. The sun was streaming through into our living room as we stared at the black and white screen. It was an amazing achievement but after about half an hour I was keen to return to bed. The next excitement was their successful return a couple of days later

Back to Skeggy

I don't know if Dad had already booked a return visit to the YMCA at Skegness but we returned there in the summer holidays. Steve drove Dad's old A40 and the three of us made the best we could of the break together. There was no sign of Ann from last year. The only other downside was suffering an injury during a highly competitive football game where I fell awkwardly damaging my neck. My sight went blurred for a while and I started to panic. Fortunately, Mom didn't seem too worried and I was back to normal the following morning. It was strange being on holiday without my Dad and it was to be the only time the three of us ever went away together.

Good news from far away

Mom had an aunt who moved to Canada before the war. Great Aunt Rose always wrote a couple of times a year and we had learnt that she had a husband and had two children but sadly all three had died over a number of years. Rose spent her last few years with a chap sharing two homes one being on the edge of one of the Great Lakes.

We received a letter from her lawyer informing us that she had passed away and left Mom and Aunt Joyce some jewellery and a share of the residue of her estate. It was so kind and such a boost to our meagre finances. Good old Aunt Rose. Her chap was the main beneficiary having made her last few years so cheerful.

Rough passage

Back at school and now in the 5th year with O levels looming my attitude was still, shall we say, relaxed. I needed at least four passes including English and Maths to enter the sixth form. Despite my poor performance in the summer exams I was confident of passing my favourite subject History, plus Geography, English and Maths.

At the end of September Aunt Joyce and Uncle Cyril had moved into their new bungalow in Kirk Michael on the Isle of Man and Mom was keen to visit. We went for the week at October half term and I took a set of revision cards I had bought at W H Smiths covering History and Geography. Unfortunately, after getting off the train at Lime Street station in Liverpool I realised I had left my parker coat on the train with my revision cards in the pockets. It was too late to turn back and despite contacting the lost property office the parker and cards were never seen again.

It was the last week in October and the sea was rough even at the quayside. As the old boat moved into the exposed Irish Sea the waves grew as did the feeling of nausea. Strange sounds came from below deck, but it soon became loud and clear that we were carrying a large number of cattle. As the boat lurched, I could hear the cattle stomping from one side to the other accompanied by distressed mooing. Many people were suffering but Mom and I managed to survive the journey without parting with any of the lunch we consumed before embarking.

The bungalow was at the head of a cul de sac in a small village a few miles north of Peel. It struck me as a little remote, particularly as my Aunt did not drive and there was just one small village shop and a deserted looking pub (the Mitre). The detached bungalow had three bedrooms, but they were using the smallest as a dining room which meant I shared a bed with Uncle Cyril. Aunt Joyce gave me careful instructions to cope with his snoring; "If he starts snoring tell him to turn and face the window". There wasn't a window on that side but there had been one at their old house and amazingly it worked.

It was a quiet week with no cards to revise from, but we had some trips out around the island and Mom enjoyed spending time with her sister. The sea was calm as we returned. I was soon back at school with only a few weeks to go before the 'O' level "mocks" started. My confidence began to suffer as reality began to sink in.

The grand Yew Tree takes shape

The Yew Tree pub now looked very different. The front entrance had been moved and the outdoor transferred to a separate shop in Hobmoor Road run by my friend Tez's mum. The biggest change was the addition of a function room called the "Rio Grande" built on the Stoney Lane side. The bowling green was now a substantial car park.

We were not quite old enough to enter the pub but discovered an abandoned van in the new car park which amused us for a short time. The car park was on a slight incline and when there was no one around we would push the van up and take it in turns to steer it back down. It didn't take long for the police to turn up and spoil the fun. The van was a wreck and had probably been left as scrap. When they arrived, Tez was in the driver's seat and being six inches taller than any of us was assumed to be our leader. When asked for his name he hesitated and slowly revealed Terence Twinberrow. They took some convincing much to our amusement. They simply told us to clear off and leave the van to be dealt with. In future years we would go beyond the car park and make full use of the pub and the Rio.

In our spare time

Other than playing lots of football we spent many hours playing Monopoly and Wembley board games. We also started to play cards for small amounts of cash. Steve was keen on playing Subbuteo, the football game involving the flicking of small figures. I was constantly accused (correctly) of pushing the figures which was against the rules. Before Subbuteo arrived Steve and my Dad spent many happy times playing Soccerette, a football game involving small players moved along the plastic surface by sticks with magnets attached. As the nights drew in a change of direction occurred.

Gaz's Mom was a regular customer at a local hairdressing salon. She usually made her appointments on Saturdays due to work. There was a young Saturday girl called Pat who also lived on Stoney Lane. Gaz's Mom became a match maker and arranged for Pat to meet up with her son. Pat had a friend called Karen who came along to the "hook up". The first meeting was at Tez's just a couple of doors down from Gaz's. They sat in the front room listening to endless plays of "Build me up Buttercup" by the Foundations. Pretty soon the gathering expanded and I was included, bringing "I want you back" by the Jackson 5. This addition just about doubled the record collection but at least they were two good songs. All pretty innocent but at least our snogging was picking up!

Other events in 1969

January 1- Space Hopper toy introduced

January 30- Beatles perform together for the last time on the roof of Apple records

March 25- John Lennon marries Yoko Ono just two weeks after Paul McCartney marries Linda Eastman

April 1- Harrier jump jet enters service with RAF

April 24- Long running radio series "Mrs Dale's diary" ends

May 23- The Who release concept album "Tommy"

July 12- Tony Jacklin wins British Open Golf

July 23- BBC launch "Pot Black". Most viewers still watching in black and white.

August 14- British troops deployed in Northern Ireland to restore order

October 5- Monty Python hits screen on BBC

November 16- Clangers launched on children's TV

November 15- John Lennon returns his MBE in protest at the Vietnam war

December 15- Martins Bank bought by Barclays

Old Yardley became the first area of Birmingham to be granted conservation status.

Castle Vale, one of the largest housing estates in Europe is completed in Birmingham

Best-selling UK single in 1969 was "Sugar Sugar" by the "virtual" group the Archies, staying at number one for 8 weeks

Chapter 14 1970:   Not too bad

Dear Diary

From the first day of the New Year I kept a diary and I continued recording every day for the next five years. The first entry records the previous night's New Year party at the Yardley's in Vicarage road. This was not the first or the last time Steve and I attended the annual event at the home of the lovely family who were close relatives of our next-door neighbours the Beresfords.

Mocks arrive

I should have spent most of the Christmas break revising for the "O level mock exams. The penny still hadn't dropped and I thought I could stroll through them. Books had been opened but not for long.

I came away from the exams thinking I had just about done enough. When the results came through I had not reached 50% in any of the subjects. My best result was 46% in Geography closely followed by History, English and Maths all in the 40's. Despite a few home truths in the school report that followed I summed it up in my diary as "Not Too Bad". Still cocky and overconfident I put the exams behind me and began to enjoy myself.

Parties with no jelly

I was sixteen years old and my hair was just over my collar even after returning from a trim at Vic Kent's barbers on Church Road opposite Woolworths. I was all set for my first party at school friend Mark Ford's where jelly was replaced by beer. There were no parents present either. We had to queue up patiently on a concrete staircase waiting for the all clear as Mark's Mom and Dad left for the pub via the staircase at the other end of the building. It was a challenge to remain silent and prevent the Party Seven cans of beer from clanging on the wall.

Mark and his slightly older brother Paul lived in a maisonette above a row of shops on Tile Cross Road.

When the all clear was declared the Ford brothers ushered us in. The music was great, particularly the introduction to the group Free featuring singer Paul Rodgers and guitarist Paul Kossoff. Not only was there a supply of beer but there were also GIRLS. My diary summed it up as "4 pints and Yvonne". I am sure the number of pints was an exaggeration as I was no drinker, however Yvonne was real enough. She was an attractive girl but a snog revealed the after taste of smoking which was a definite turn off. She was there with her friend Elaine Jenkins who I was also attracted to.

Clubbing it

Yvonne and Elaine told us they went to a youth club at Christ Church on Burney Lane Ward End. Elaine went to Saltley Grammar school and told us that many of her school friends also went to the club as did some of my Central school friends. I turned up with friends Gaz, Tez and Bri and so did Yvonne. I stayed well away concentrating on table tennis and snooker on the smallest table I had ever seen. Fortunately, we mixed well with the Saltley girls and I was particularly taken by Elaine. We were delighted to be invited to an under 18's disco at the BRS (British Road Services) on Bromford Lane set for the very next day.

Amazingly entrance to the BRS was free as it was the first week. It was packed and Elaine and I clicked straight away. We had fun dancing the night away to hits such Edison lighthouse's "Love grows where my Rosemary goes". This was the start of a relationship between two youngsters that would be on and off for the next couple of years.

More parties without jelly

Parties at people's houses became a frequent event with the very next one at Elaine's on Sheldon Heath Road. The first thing that struck me was the colour television. I didn't know anyone with one. Although it was meant to be a party the lads were soon watching the rugby purring over the colour of the grass! The next person I would know to have a colour TV would be Grandpa Duffin a couple of years later. In the meantime I would be back to Elaine's for both the FA Cup and World Cup finals.

My diary confirms that there were a total of fourteen parties in 1970 held by ten different people. The Fords hosted three of them.

'O' levels approach

I was enjoying seeing a lot of Elaine. The youth club was held every Tuesday and bravely held occasional discos on Saturdays. We went to the BRS a few more times where a charge had now been introduced. We also went to other youth clubs at Long Meadow school and Rowlands Road.

Was my schoolwork affected? Probably no more than it would have been with my new social life. I had done very little revision for the mocks and the real thing was not forcing me to up my game.

Two other events didn't help. Firstly, our teachers withdrew their labour on several occasions in the weeks leading up to the exams. I don't blame them as they were not well paid at the time and I don't think I can attribute my results to this.

The second seems a little odd now. Our good family friends the Muddimans invited my mum and I to join them for a week in a caravan at Abersoch on the Welsh coast. The only problem was that this was a week before the 'O' levels began. I was delighted as I liked their daughter Julia who was a year younger in age but far more mature than young Duffin. It was an enjoyable break but not good preparation for the upcoming exams as no books were taken with me.

I thought the exams in my five key subjects went OK with the exception of Geology which I found quite tough. The results came by telegram from Steve as Mom and I were on holiday at Aunt Joyce and Uncle Cyril's on the Isle of Man. I had only passed English and Geography. No sixth form for me! I would have to repeat the fifth year and retake the exams. The penny was finally dropping!

Pubs discovered

Underage drinking was a lot more common back then with proof of age rarely, if ever, asked for. My first purchase was at the White House hotel in Abersoch. On holiday with Muddimans, their daughter Julia had asked me to take her into the centre of Abersoch one evening. I was delighted to accompany her but more than a little nervous of entering a bar let alone having to make my first alcoholic purchase in front of her. Fortunately, all went well and I mentally ticked another first.

Just a couple of weeks later after sitting one of the Maths papers Mark Ford and I decided to go for a pint at the Ring O Bells (AKA the Ringers) on Church Road. This was the first of literally hundreds of visits to the Ringers over the next few years. Landlord Sam and wife Jean were extremely tolerant of their young customers. On some Friday evenings the Assembly room would host up to twenty youngsters, many underage and drinking very little.

Another job at the CO-OP

With the cricket season approaching I decided to leave the Pool Way supermarket and try to establish myself back in the cricket team. It was harder than I thought but I did manage to play for both the first and second elevens. However, my batting was literally hit and miss.

When the school cricket finished, I asked for Uncle Peter's help again for another job at the CO-OP. As I had finished school after the exams I was free for about eight weeks until school started again. He was really helpful and found me a job at the CO-OP Oak restaurant in the basement of the High Street Store. The manager was the affable and well-spoken Dennis Downing who was a friend and colleague of my late Dad. I remembered him from when I used to help out serving pop at the Sports club's annual gala.

It was a totally different role to filling shelves at the supermarket. The hardest work was manning the dish washing machine. It was a cross between a train set and a miniature car wash. About half a dozen trays packed with crockery moved along the circuit passing through a tunnel where water was sprayed along with detergent. There was another tunnel drying the clean goods but adding hot air to the already baking kitchen. There were two or three other part time lads and we had a lot of fun as well as working hard. Picking up a whole week's wages was a real boost which enabled me to buy new clothes including a Wrangler jacket and treat Elaine to the pictures.

Popping round to Mothers

My friend Mark Ford had now left school and asked me if I wanted to go to a club in Erdington that was a fantastic venue for bands he liked. I jumped at the chance. The first band we saw was Gentle Giant. I had never heard of them but was told that they were formed from the more well-known Simon Dupree and the Big Sound who had a top ten single called Kites.

It was probably due to GG being my first live band but I loved them and went on to buy several of their albums after Elaine had bought me their first at Christmas.

Mothers was above a furniture shop but some of our greatest bands performed there including Pink Floyd, Fleetwood Mac, Free, The Who, Led Zeppelin, Yes, Black Sabbath, Family, and many more. About six months after my first visit the club was forced to close at the beginning of 1971 with Elton John being the penultimate act. I went four times including seeing Eric Clapton perform with Derek and the Dominoes. Great to see Clapton but the room was boiling hot due to overcrowding. The band kept leaving the stage due to the heat and we ran out of time as we needed to catch the last number 11 bus home.

In September we started to see bands at the Town Hall. The first two were Procol Harum and Jethro Tull. These were soon followed by Taste, Free and Mott the Hoople. This was the start of seeing 40 bands whilst I was still at school.

Back to school

I knew that I would have to repeat the fifth year and resit the exams I had failed. What I didn't realise was that I would have to also resit the two I had passed. This meant I had to attend all the lessons as well. The good news was I could add two new subjects; English literature and British Constitution. The other good news was that I could resit some subjects after Christmas.
I was still at a loss as to how I had failed History as I had finished 10th out of 40 in the mocks. It turned out that surprisingly very few had passed the exam. Today there would have been an appeal as something was clearly wrong.

Puppy love

Elaine and I had a wobble in August but after a short break we were back together. We were very young, and I was probably a little bit flippant about things as I discovered the adventures associated with growing up. I was now going to pubs more often but Elaine was younger and although very attractive would not pass the age test easily although we did manage to go to the Parisian a few times. This led to me not spending as much time with Elaine as I should have.

John Lavender and I discovered the Alhambra pub in town. We could not believe how good it was. It was a basement pub with great music and a lively atmosphere. It was so crowded I eventually took Elaine there.

The Yew Tree pub was only a couple of hundred yards from the end of our road and had a relatively new function suite called the Rio Grande. It held a disco on Sunday evenings and for some time had been a venue for "bobbers" and skinheads. However, it changed to more our kind of music i.e. Progressive Rock (Prog Rock) calling the Sunday night disco 'Sabbath Rock'. The boys went regularly with Elaine and her friend Fiona joining us at Christmas when it was ticket only.

We did see quite a few films including Easy Rider, which we saw twice. Butch Cassidy and the Sundance kid was a great film. Planet of the Apes was interesting, particularly the ending.

A memorable year ended back where it started at the Yardley's New Party. If I had learned one thing it was the importance of hard work at school. You don't get "owt for nowt" as they say in Yorkshire.

Other events in 1970

January 1- Age of Majority lowered from 21 to 18

January 1- Merger of National Provincial and Westminster banks to form the National Westminster bank

January 22- First Jumbo Jet (Boeing747) lands in Britain

February 13- Black Sabbath launch their first album entitled "Black Sabbath"

March 23 - 23 victims of Thalidomide awarded nearly £370,000

April 1- Paul McCartney leaves the Beatles

May 22- South African cricket team withdraw from tour after threats from other countries to withdraw from the Commonwealth Games

June 19- Conservatives win General Election under Ted Heath

July 31- Last serving of "grog" in the Royal Navy

August 9- Notting Hill riots

September 18- Jimi Hendrix dies of drug related heart attack

September19- First Glastonbury Festival held with T REX the headline act replacing the Kinks who pulled out

October 19- BP discovers large oil field in the North Sea

November 21- Gay Liberation Front
held their first march

December 26- Athlete Lillian Board, 22, dies in Munich

Richard Branson launches the Virgin Group

Best-selling single in 1970 was Elvis Presley "The Wonder of You" remaining at Number 1 for six weeks.

There were some memorable songs released including All Right Now, Paranoid, Black Night, Bridge over Troubled Water, Spirit in the Sky, I hear you knocking, Lola, Layla, Let's work together and In the Summertime. Also, some unusual hits such as Wandering Star, Two Little Boys and Grooving with Mr Bloe.

Difficult to select a favourite but I saw Layla performed by Derek and the Dominos at Mothers and Free perform All Right Now at three gigs. I will leave it there.

Chapter 15 1971: Off to work we go

Make your mind up Paul

Attractive, intelligent and a great sense of humour. What else could I wish for? I did not have an answer. Elaine and I were on and off through the whole year due to me frequently changing my mind. Poor girl. We did have a lot of good times seeing many great bands, films and having fun with friends. Despite this I did not always treat Elaine well.

The harder you work

Repeating the 5th year was never going to be easy. I had finally realised that more work was required and put in many hours revision before resitting the History exam in January. I was also enjoying the two new subjects and was determined to do well in the mocks.

When the results came out I was disappointed to fail again in Maths and Geology resits. It was not all bad news as my History failure had turned into a top-grade A pass. This added to the mystery of my earlier result.

The two mocks went really well with me sailing through British Constitution with the highest mark. English Literature was almost as good as I secured the second highest mark. At the end of March I now had three 'O' levels in the bag.

In June I finally passed Maths and the two new subjects bringing my 'O' level total to six subjects. I also passed English and Geography the two subjects I was forced to take again despite having passed them the previous year.

The Main Chance

At the previous year's career interview I was asked how tall I was. Fortunately, I was below average height at the time and discussions about entering the police force came to a close.

This time it was different as the first question asked was what television programmes did I enjoy? Without really thinking I responded with "The Main Chance". It starred the actor John Stride as a solicitor who flourished when he moved from London to Leeds.

As a result It was suggested that I might think of becoming a Legal Executive which was the updated title for Managing Clerks. I liked the sound of that and waited to see if I would be interviewed at the Law Society in Temple Street.

I didn't have to wait long to be invited. I also went for interviews at the Civil Service and Local Authority housing department. The Law Society interview went very well and made the other two meetings seem quite dull. I was told by the Law Society that if successful my details would be passed on to Solicitor firms in the city centre.

Both the Civil Service and Housing Department offered me a job but I was after the main chance.

I was interviewed by two senior partners at Wragge & Co, one of the largest firms outside London. It could not have gone better and my letter of appointment soon followed. I was to attend a two-week course at the Law Society at the beginning of September. I was delighted. I did make one mistake as I assumed that I would start at the firm after the course however it turned out that the other three trainees started in July. This meant I unnecessarily worked at the CO-OP restaurant throughout the summer.

It's fun to stay at the YMCA

Skegness was easily my favourite YMCA holiday centre I had visited with my parents and John and Gaz were keen to give it a try. My Mom had retained her membership and a week in August was booked. Our coach booking was made at the Dorothy Box and John's Dad took us to the its departure point at the Fox and Goose.

It was a great week made interesting by meeting up with four lovely girls from Bradford. I fell for Lynn after briefly aligning with her friend Linda. There was a particularly tense period when Lynn's boyfriend turned up with a couple of his pals and struck Lynn. We didn't see it happen although we did see how upset Lynn was afterwards. She thought they had finished before she came on holiday. They certainly were after that.

After we came home I went to Bradford and Lynn came down to Brum for my 18th birthday. When Lynn said she was thinking of joining the army and would be training in the Midlands I decided this was too much too soon and ended it.

I have to confess I was seeing Elaine in between all of this, well on and off.

The real work starts

The course was interesting and the other dozen trainees were a friendly bunch. The lecturers included the partner I would be assigned to at Wragges. John Duncombe (JHD) was a small rather dapper chap with glasses and dark hair. He struck me as very professional but not a lot of fun. I was right.

When I turned up at the offices in Windsor House close to Rackhams department store I was shown into JHD's office. He gave me a friendly welcome and explained I would be focused on conveyancing (buying and selling houses). My desk was right outside his office. The training was really seeking help from other solicitors and Legal Exec's in his team. His secretary Ann was a great help to me.

All the trainees from the course signed up for tuition towards the Legal Executive exams at Matthew Boulton college off Broad street. I was soon in the flow and enjoying work.

Rio sent to Coventry

There was a shock in October when the DJ announced there was both good news and bad news. The bad news was that due to poor drink sales the pub was shutting down Sabbath Rock. The good news was that it was moving to the Sportsman Arms on the Coventry Road with a free coach provided. Net result; carry on as usual with no further to walk. It turned out Ok especially when I found myself with the very pretty Glynis

A brief moment of fame

The timing of hooking up with Glynis was fortuitous. I was in an off spell with Elaine although she was at the Sportsman's that evening. I also had two tickets for the live performance of Braden's Week (later became That's Life) at BBC Pebble Mill for the following Saturday. On the Friday I sacrificed seeing Elton John at the Town Hall to take Glynis out for a drink at the White Hart on Tile Cross Road. Things seemed to be going well.

When we arrived at Pebble Mill we queued up to enter the studio. As we reached the entrance Glynis and I were removed from the general line and taken in the opposite direction and instructed to sit behind the desks where the presenters would sit. I had no doubt that it was down to Glynis's attractive features that we would be right behind the presenters and in full view of the camera.

Esther Rantzen sat right in front of us and when covering a story about Birmingham chip shops she turned to us and offered us a chip. It was a great night, but the delight didn't last.

I had agreed to meet Glynis the following night but when I. arrived at her house I was handed a note. It was a "Dear John letter". I had been dumped. I was furious. I had given up seeing Elton John, had got her on television and she didn't even have the heart to tell me herself. I tried to get in touch but to no avail. I think that her previous boyfriend who had "wheels" (a Van) was back on the scene and the attraction of a Birmingham Corporation was no contest. Now I knew how Elaine had felt.

That's entertainment

My friend John Lavender's Mom Doreen was a real character and we got on well. She worked as a cashier at the ABC cinema on New Street. Her job entitled her to a pass for two free tickets per week. John and I used them most weeks. If a film was retained for a second week John would sometimes generously give the pass to me to take a "friend".

I went to thirty music gigs in 1971. Mostly at the Town Hall but also at the Mayfair Suite and the Odeon New Street. We also went to more local venues such as The Hideaway, Harlequin plus the Swan and Bulls Head pubs. We saw some top bands including Led Zeppelin, Deep Purple, Free, Family, the Faces, Emerson Lake and Palmer, Curved Air, King Crimson, and the Who.

I was out most nights. Our fall-back venue was the Ring O Bells (AKA the Ringers). If I stayed in I would listen to my growing record collection or watch television. Star Trek was still a favourite of mine. A new American western "alias Smith and Jones" caught my attention. Although I had grown up with westerns this show cleverly added humour. For pure comedy there was still Morecombe and Wise. The second series of the controversial Monty Python's Flying Circus was essential viewing for my age group. Sport was still free to view and I keenly watched all the main events.

Back at the Yardley's

Another eventful year ends with friends and family at the Yardley's on New Year's Eve. Exams had been sorted. An enjoyable job had been secured and I was no longer seeing Elaine (for now).

The last two chapters 1970 and 1971 are very much shortened versions of those contained in my first book "Not Too Bad" available from Amazon with all royalties donated to Guide Dogs UK.

Other events in 1971

January 2nd - Ibrox disaster. 66 crushed to death at football match between Rangers and Celtic

February 15th - Decimal currency introduced

March 8th - Postal strike ends after 47 days

April 19th - Unemployment reaches a post war high of 815,000

May 11th - The Daily Sketch newspaper is withdrawn and absorbed by the Daily Mail

June 24th - The EEC agrees terms for UK membership

July 1st - Sunday Bloody Sunday released. The first mainstream British film with a bisexual theme

August 15th - Show jumper Harvey Smith stripped of his victory after using the V sign

September 21st -The television music show the Old Grey Whistle Test aired on BBC2

October 31st - Bomb explodes at the top of the Post office Tower

November 10th - Spaghetti junction opens

December 30th - Diamonds are Forever released starring Sean Connery in his final Bond role

Also

Inflation stood at a 30 year high at 8.6%

Oil overtook coal as the most used fuel in the UK

Spike Milligan's "Adolph Hitler, my part in his downfall" and Frederick Forsyth's "Day of the Jackal" released (I bought and read them both)

Uk's bestselling single in 1971 My Sweet Lord by George Harrison spent five weeks at Number 1

Epilogue: The big changes

I have enjoyed reliving my early years in Brum and being able to compare it to the modern day. Some say that nostalgia is not what it used to be but I found telling my story both illuminating and heart-warming. We now live in a very different world but is it better or worse? It is impossible to be certain and I am a great believer in life being a balance with there nearly always being an upside to every downside.

Standard of living

I can start with a relatively easy one. Our standard of living has improved since the 1950's but not at an even pace. I have used Hillarys.co.uk to compare some current day facts with the West Midlands "Back in the day" 1957 when this book starts:

1. Housing

The average house price in the West Midlands was just above £2000 which would be about £45,000 in today's prices. The average price for a house in Birmingham today is £230,000. Home ownership was in the low 30% region compared to today's 65%. Much of this is down to the sale of council houses but is also the result of the huge growth of lending encouraged by government. As I ended my career being responsible for mortgages at the Halifax, the UK's largest lender, I have to support the benefits of the huge rise in home ownership.

However, the trend has seen a reversal in recent years with first time buyers struggling to get on the property ladder. The number of under 30 year olds staying at home has therefore risen substantially.

When it comes to our home comforts there have been many improvements. Central heating is now widespread. Toilets are indoors and the pipes rarely freeze. Double glazing and increased insulation help keep the cold out. My own experience has certainly been very positive. I remember telling my Mom that when I had my own house the hot water would always be available and there would be no ice on the inside of the windows. Fortunately, I was correct.

2. Work

The mid 1950's was a period of full employment which is pretty much where we are today despite some huge peaks in unemployment in the 70's and 80's. The average salary in 1957 was £489 (worth about £11,000 today) compared to today's average of just under £30,000 (2019). Manufacturing has declined with the service sector expanding.

By the time I started work in 1971 the job market was buoyant and I had the choice of three careers. It is much tougher today to find career roles, with lower paid unskilled jobs more prevalent. Apprenticeships are trying to make a comeback against a background of increased automation and declining manufacturing.

Wages are more out of kilter. At the lower end the minimum wage is trying to protect the low paid. At the other end the pay of CEO's and other senior employees has gone off the scale. Gone are the days when the Prime Minister's pay could be used as some sort of benchmark. It is difficult to buy the argument that exorbitant salaries need to be paid to attract the right calibre of executive.

3. Cars

There are now almost 40 million licensed vehicles on the roads of Great Britain compared to 4 million in 1950. This is a major cause of pollution particularly from diesel fumes.

In 1967 the average car cost around £740 (equivalent to £16,724) about 21% less than today. A litre of fuel was equivalent to £1.26 which is not much less than current prices (2019) cost. Many families now boast more than one car on their drive.

There have been huge advances in the design of cars. Gone are the rust buckets that I drove in the early 1970's. Cars are more reliable and safer to drive with heaters that work and can be set to separately heat driver and passenger. The developments required for driverless cars are already improving safety with features to control the likes of distance from the vehicle in front and lane position.

The impact of climate change is forcing a move towards electric cars and away from petrol and diesel. As someone with severe sight impairment I wonder whether I will ever sit in a driverless vehicle? Definitely an improving area despite the problems with pollution.

Moving to other areas

Community spirit

I have lived in the same street in Wetherby for the last 28 years. This is longer than the 26 years I lived in Brum of which 25 years were in Charminster Avenue. Now I only know the people who live in the next three houses on either side, whereas I can still name virtually everyone who lived in Charminster Avenue and a good number of those who lived in Rockingham and Heathmere. Due to poor sight I have not been able to drive since 2002 so regularly walk along our street, I cannot remember the last time I met someone along the way. It was never like that back in Brum. We were very close to neighbours often calling them aunts and uncles. Sadly, much of this has gone.

This is partly due to car ownership but also to more people working away from home particularly women as the family roles are more equally shared. The sense of community has not completely gone but it has weakened. Have to put this down as worse.

Communication

This has improved so much that it has caused problems we could never have imagined. The internet has improved knowledge and awareness but at the same time social media has potentially damaged the lives of many vulnerable people particularly youngsters. Mobile phones have virtually done away with the need to plan ahead and arrangements are often made or changed at the last minute. As a deafblind person I would be lost without my phone and the ability to make words huge on my Apple Mac and read my Kindle with the font size on maximum. Despite the problem of Trolls, I judge this as a plus with issues.

Sport

The huge influx of money has affected most sports. None more so than football. Top players earning over £300k PER WEEK have crossed the line from well paid to obscene. Even the average for Premier League players has passed £50,000 per week. The ironic thing is that whilst I am a critic it is partly my fault as I subscribe to SKY Sports, the source of much of the funding. There is no doubt that performance levels have improved but at what cost.

It is not just money and professionalism that have affected sport. Performance enhancing drugs have made major inroads into athletics and cycling to name just two. Despite the downsides I have to give it a thumbs up as a sports fan to the increased performance and television coverage.

Health

We live longer thanks to a combination of diet, medication and improved medical knowledge. It is not all good news as obesity and pollution have grown to worrying levels. Junk food is all too common and traffic fumes have risen with the growing number of vehicles.

The NHS struggles to cope with rising demand caused by the numbers of people living longer and the development of new services and treatments. My experience of the NHS due to my disabilities has been excellent but key functions such as A&E are under tremendous pressure. There is good news as time spent in recovery is now far less thanks to medical advances. I spent more than a week recovering in hospital from an appendix operation back in 1957, today it would be one or two days. A hernia operation a couple of years ago had me going home the same day. Although I walked around like a 90 year old for a couple of weeks.

In 1962 70% of men smoked. The current level has plummeted to 15%. In the same year a landmark report confirmed the link between smoking and lung cancer. The banning of advertising, smoking in public places and increased tax have also helped lower the uptake.

Our health is certainly better but there are still many areas that need support as we live longer.

Music

Sadly I have not been able to recognise any music for the last few years due my deafness. Growing up with the Beatles and Stones before moving through progressive rock to a more balanced approach to music gave me a wide exposure. I am in no real position to judge the current music scene just feel lucky to have experienced the birth and development of popular music. Seeing 40 live bands whilst still at school now seems remarkable.

The platforms for playing and hearing music have developed from vinyl, tape, eight tracks, CDs, to streaming using iPods and iPads and now smart phones. I know I am biased but if it is just the music itself, I am going for "better then".

Holidays

The YMCA family holiday centres have gone but Butlins (now 3 camps), Pontins (6) and Warners (14 hotels) are all still going albeit aiming at different markets to the 1950's and 60's. Package holidays abroad pretty much killed the holiday camp offer and the main players cut back and refocused.

Air travel has grown incredibly with well over 3 billion passengers in 2016. Since the introduction of jet planes in the 1950's the cost of travel has reduced substantially as competition expanded. The world has been opened up for many people to experience different cultures and the beauty of our incredibly diverse planet.

One of the downsides has been the negative impact on many traditional UK resorts such as Blackpool and Scarborough. Many are now home to people on benefits with far fewer families visiting with buckets and spades.

Overall this is an area that has improved for the most part both in terms of choice and cost.

Education

My school reports show my primary class size at 45. Secondary education was much better with class size down to 30 when I entered Central Grammar. The 11+ was introduced in 1944 as a method of selection based on examination at age 11. The system was largely withdrawn in the 1970's and replaced in many areas with comprehensive (no selection) schools.

Nowadays class sizes are closer to 30 at all levels and the structure of teaching is much more flexible towards pupil needs. However, there are still major funding and pupil testing issues across the board. The role of teachers has moved more towards curriculum delivery and results however I tip this slightly in favour of improved.

Politics

My Dad was from a staunch Labour supporting family. In fact, Grandpa Duffin came back from his four years of service in the First World War leaning towards communism (or was it "Lenin" towards it!). In recent years the main political parties have done a disservice to democracy. My Dad would be very critical of Labour's move away from its traditional roots. Not that the other parties have performed any better. I have always encouraged my own offspring to at least use their votes. Given the way the first past the post works it is increasingly difficult to stand firmly behind the current system.

Gender

It is not surprising that many of our youngsters are confused about their orientation. There is now so much pressure to consider your direction that confusion must abound. Non-gender specific loos are becoming widespread even in some schools. Back in the 50's boys would be boys and girls would be girls. This is a very difficult and complex area particularly helping those affected by transgender issues. The good news it is no longer hidden as it was simpler back in the 50's largely due to our ignorance although I am sure there was some burying of truth. I hope as knowledge improves we will cope with this area far better.

Political correctness (PC)

Oh boy! I end on another tough one. PC was not recognised in the 1950's and did not really surface as a serious description until the 1980's. It is easy to look back and judge at those times using today's understanding and perspective.

What we have to remember is that the climate was totally different. My parents were not racist but they loved the "Black and White Minstrels Show" without thinking about race. Yes, there was some language used by many people that would make you cringe today. For example, the 1960 Rupert Bear annual had Rupert visiting "Coon island" which was inhabited by little black "Coons". The use of words such as coon and wog were common and often used as sloppy or poor descriptions rather than abuse, although that happened too.

Later TV programmes such as "Curry and Chips", "Love thy Neighbour" and "Mind your language" would quite rightly have no chance of being televised today. Although it is easy to be judgemental from a distance and PC does sometimes go way over the top it is a force blowing in the right direction.

Sexism was all too common back in the 1950's and 60's. Even when I started work at the Leeds in 1974 none of the 400 branches were managed by women. Now the majority of Halifax branches are run by women. There are still large areas of inequality, but things are improving. The gender pay gap is closing but still there in many areas.

Homophobia was also commonplace back in the 1950's and 60's with homosexuality not becoming decriminalised until 1967. I remember "homo" jokes being told at school. I don't think we knew the harm these would cause people. I had a very good friend who I had no idea was gay until I was in my early twenties. He must have gone through hell. It is not perfect today but with civil partnerships and now marriage available things are much more open and accepted.

An improving area although sometimes it becomes overstretched particularly when looking back at yesteryear using today's accepted values and ignoring those that were prevalent at the time.

In conclusion I feel both lucky and privileged to have been part of the generation born in the post war years. No wars to fight, increasing medical advances, a solid education and many career opportunities and being able to afford a house at 25. I am a very grateful Baby Booming Brummie.

If you have enjoyed this book you may also enjoy my book NOT TOO BAD based on my diaries from the start of 1970 to the end on 1974. It goes into far more detail than the overlap in the years 1970/71 covered here. It has already raised over £1,500 for Guide Dogs UK and is on sale at Amazon at a reduced price (£5 Nov 2019).

Printed in Poland
by Amazon Fulfillment
Poland Sp. z o.o., Wrocław